UNVEILING SATAN'S PLAN TO DESTROY AMERICA

HOW GOD WILL DELIVER THE USA

DAVID HOPE

Unveiling Satan's Plan to Destroy America:
How God Will Deliver the USA
Copyright © 2016 by David Hope

All rights reserved. No part of this book may be reproduced or transmitted in any form or by any means without written permission of the author.

ISBN-13: 978-0-9981829-0-2

Printed in the United States of America

RevMedia Publishing
PO BOX 5172, Kingwood, TX 77325
www.revmediapublishing.com

Unless otherwise indicated, Scripture quotations are taken from the King James Version of the Bible.

Scripture quotations marked NIV are taken from THE HOLY BIBLE, NEW INTERNATIONAL VERSION®, NIV® Copyright © 1973, 1978, 1984, 2011 by Biblica, Inc.® Used by permission. All rights reserved worldwide.

CONTENTS

INTRODUCTION 9

CHAPTER ONE 21
God Gave Us Capitalism

CHAPTER TWO 31
The Origin of Modern Socialism

CHAPTER THREE 45
Learning from History

CHAPTER FOUR 63
Cloward and Piven: Setting the Stage for Alinsky's *Rules for Radicals*

CHAPTER FIVE 73
Saul Alinsky and *Rules for Radicals*

CHAPTER SIX 83
Cloward and Piven's Dream Comes True

CHAPTER SEVEN 95
Agenda 21 and Phony Environmentalism

CHAPTER EIGHT 111
Agenda 21 Companions: Common Core and Planned Parenthood

CHAPTER NINE 121
How to Defeat Satan's Plan

ENDNOTES 133

WHAT OTHERS ARE SAYING

Pastor David, your book, *Unveiling Satan's Plan to Destroy America*, is simply outstanding. Your chapter on the origins of socialism in the Fabian Society is worth the whole book. Every minister and business and political leader in America should have a copy of this book and should study it chapter by chapter. You state your fully supported case in the most succinct, compelling and explosive way.

Your continued exposure of political elites who follow the doctrine of Saul Alinsky is also admirable. His doctrine follows the same logic as that of Nicolo Machiavelli in Renaissance Europe who insisted that the only value is power and that any means to obtain it and retain it is acceptable.

A related doctrine also follows the thesis that manufactured chaos is the precedent for social transformation. This is the modus operandi of all socialist revolutionaries. Manufactured chaos can take an innocuous form such as governmentally complicated forms of doing business that essentially strangle productivity and profitability out of existence. In doing this a society becomes chaotic through impoverishment.

Your opening chapter that demonstrates the overt Christian character of the United States during what you call "the founding period" of 1760-1805 is also admirable since it tells the truth. Your love for America has re-inspired me. I wish you and this very fine book the very best success possible. And with you I pray for and believe for God's intervention through his people and the Gospel of our Lord Jesus Christ to set the captive Free!

Dr. Bron Barkley
Founding Pastor of Shalom Hebraic Christian Congregation
Kingwood, TX

Somebody needed to write this book, *Unveiling Satan's Plan to Destroy America*. God chose David Hope. He has clearly done his homework before deliberating these truths. I don't see how he could have made it any clearer to a reader. There are two ways to view things, God's way - or fallen humanity's way. David has clearly shown both opposing views. Thank you, David, for presenting such a work of meditation, care and love in your approach. It is a timely message that America, and the world, so desperately needs today.

The reader will not waste his time reading this warning to a nation so deeply in need of this knowledge. This book should be a best seller.

Gerald Davis DD
Gerald Davis Ministries
New Caney, TX

Author David Hope has done it again! When I received his invitation to write a review for *Unveiling Satan's Plan to Destroy America*, I thought to myself, 'I hope this manuscript isn't going to be one of those crazy conspiracy books!' Upon further reflection I realized that Bible clearly reveals that Satan does have a conspiracy to dethrone God and destroy anything on planet earth that reflects His nature and character. Call it 'strategy' or 'conspiracy', America is one of his prime targets. I agree with Hope. Satan does, in fact, want to destroy America.

Mr. Hope provides diverse and factual research and then connects the dots. You will be amazed how the author skillfully draws his fascinating conclusions from various world views. He then draws powerful insights from relevant passages in the Bible.

I was both enlightened and challenged as I read this amazing book. I think you will as well.

C.E.. Buddy Hicks, D. Min.
Humble, TX

After reading David Hope's newest book, *Unveiling Satan's Plan to Destroy America*, yeah, the second time, I am convinced that certain of our nation's public leadership (and those that are clandestine) are in collusion with Satan directly. And that collusion is to destroy our blessed nation and to create a global government.

Indeed, the author educates the reader fully through history of nations that have lost all through communism, socialism, and the removal of Christianity. I am especially taken aback by how our governmental leadership has inoculated our politics and society with anti American and socialistic views with intent to destroy the freedoms of enterprise and capitalism.

However, in reading this book, I am almost enraged as I am educated by the author concerning the overt strategy of liberalism to force government control through the radical, Luciferian writings of one Saul Alinsky. Most especially affected by the teaching and writing of Alinsky is presidential candidate Hillary Rodham Clinton, who became a devoted follower of his writings. The author warns us that if the Alinsky doctrines through liberalism and Clinton are to be implemented into our country and yes, the entire world, it will intersperse a socialistic collectivism that will take every hope of pursuit of happiness you have ever entertained.

Had not author David Hope provided hope through the word of God and prophecies for our future, I would be terrified as to my future as an American and a Christian. The propaganda and perverted science concerning global warming and environmental concerns provided by this government is nothing more, David Hope shares, than the organized process of taking control of every company and citizen, and yes, every nation of the world. Adherence to environment has become law through great deceptions. When President Obama stated that the greatest enemy we have before us is global warming and the decline of environment, I was shocked. What of ISIS? What of nuclear capabilities of Iran and North Korea? What of the joblessness of our country?

Surely, as author Hope provides, there is a concerted effort of human leadership and Satan to overthrow our nation as we know it today as well as the entire world. This book is a must read.

Frank Mazzapica
Pastor, New Covenant Church
Humble, TX

INTRODUCTION

When I look at the current condition of the United States of America, my heart breaks to see the decline of our nation in morals, education and the economy. Equally painful is the overwhelming lack of understanding of our real history by our citizens, particularly our young people. One of the most devastating things to reflect on is our leadership, who demonstrate not a shred of godly wisdom in operation.

At the time of this writing, July of 2016, many people believe that Barack Obama's agenda is to destroy the United States and relegate the U. S. Constitution to the ash heap of history. Is that really true or is that mere political wrangling? The answer to that question will be revealed throughout the pages of this book.

As we watch our liberties slowly being taken away from us, it is very important not to lose heart and to remember the words of Jesus in John 6:63.

It is the Spirit who gives life; the flesh profits nothing. The words that I speak to you are spirit, and they are life. (NKJV)

Living things can look like they are dead. The love of freedom in the hearts of our citizens appears to be almost dead. Americans need the life found in the Word of God sown into their hearts. During the Obama presidency, our nation has been bombarded with excessive presidential executive orders that bypass Congress. We have also experienced thousands of unreasonable, burdensome regulations that have had a crippling effect on virtually every industry. The devil, using willing participants, has been so active and so brazen in his efforts to thwart our freedoms that the faithful, godly believers in our nation seem almost dead when compared with the boldness of Satan.

It may seem to you that there is no hope in sight, as our nation looks like a bunch of dry, dead bones. America was so great when we were "one nation under God," but now look at it. So, what shall we do? Do we just wring our hands and whine and complain, or throw our hands in the air and give up?

No way! What did God tell Ezekiel to do in the valley of the dry bones? God told him to prophesy to those bones. He obeyed and prophesied to the bones and they began to live and come together as a great army to defeat the enemies of God's people.

> *Again He said to me, Prophesy to these bones, and say to them, 'O dry bones, hear the word of the Lord! Thus says the Lord God to these bones: Surely I will cause breath to enter into you, and you shall live. I will put sinews on you and bring flesh upon you, cover you with skin and put breath in you; and you shall live. Then you shall know that I am the Lord. So I prophesied as I was commanded; and as I prophesied, there was a noise, and suddenly a rattling; and the bones came together, bone to bone. Indeed, as I looked, the*

sinews and the flesh came upon them, and the skin covered them over; but there was no breath in them. Also He said to me, Prophesy to the breath, prophesy, son of man, and say to the breath, Thus says the Lord God: Come from the four winds, O breath, and breathe on these slain, that they may live. So I prophesied as He commanded me, and breath came into them, and they lived, and stood upon their feet, an exceedingly great army. (EZEKIEL 37:4-10 NKJV)

To see a turnaround in our nation, we will have to prophesy to our nation and let the words of God bring God-life and resurrection power to our land. We should declare that we are blessed and command the army of believers to live and be strong in the Lord. We should prophesy that we are one nation under God and that those in authority in all areas of influence are men and women who love Jesus, who hear the voice of the Good Shepard and will not follow any other voice.

We should further prophesy with our mouths, in the name of Jesus, that those who do not follow the voice of God will be removed from office. God's original design for this nation was for his people to be in charge and he has not changed his mind. We should proclaim that all those in authority are great people who are there to serve and not to be served, and all who are there to be served shall be removed by the people.

But he who is greatest among you shall be your servant. And whoever exalts himself will be humbled, and he who humbles himself will be exalted. (MATTHEW 23:11-12)

As a young man it was obvious to me that the people who hated God also hated Israel, Jews, and Christians.

As I got older I could see more clearly. I don't know if the devil got bolder or I got more discernment, but I could readily see that those who hated God not only hated Israel, but hated the United States as well.

In fact, Iran calls the United States "the great Satan" and Israel "little Satan." Why is that? It's because God gave our founders, by the Holy Ghost, the American free-enterprise capitalistic system so that we can be a blessing to the whole world. Later, we will discuss the various godly assignments that God has given to the United States of America.

When our free enterprise system is working properly (with very little government intrusion) people are free to make decisions on their own. The devil doesn't like that, because he wants to control people.

As I got even older, I noticed that whoever hates God, not only hates Israel, Jews, Christians, the United States and free-market capitalism, but also hates the military of the United States. Think about this. If it took natural blood to gives us spiritual freedom, how much more does it take natural blood to give and keep freedom in the physical world?

Those opposed to God and his kingdom would like to see the U. S. military held in low regard and diminished in power and influence. Why? Because a robust U.S. military confronts evil and thus frustrates many demonic strategies. Our enemy, Satan, has come against our military. He is opposed to anyone or any organization that confronts evil.

The enemy opposes pastors, missionaries and other ministers, our military, and police officers. It has now become glaringly apparent that our enemy has waged an all-out assault on police officers because of their courage to confront evil.

The devil is getting bolder, so we must get bolder in what we do for the Kingdom of God. We have to have more boldness in what we declare and we have to call things that are not as though they are.

> *...as it is written, "I have made you a father of many nations") in the presence of Him whom he believed—God, who gives life to the dead and calls those things which do not exist as though they did;* (ROMANS 4:17 NKJV*)*

Throughout this book, I will pull back the curtain on the devil's play book, some of which appears in the book *Rules for Radicals* by Saul Alinsky, which is dedicated to Lucifer. This book by Alinsky is what most of those who follow Satan primarily follow.

To make a point, I've listed below a couple of dedications from books I have in my office. I want you to contrast the kind of words that people who are serving God, bringing truth, liberty, and healing to others use as compared to the dedication of Alinsky, who served the devil.

With permission from my friend and author, David Yanez, and his publisher, Whitaker House, below please find the dedication from *Igniter of Faith*:

"I dedicate this to my father, Reverend Gabriel Yanez, Jr., who passed away too early but built a home full of faith in God and gave his family a belief in miracles."

Here is the dedication from my book, *Keep Knocking*, shown with permission from my publisher, Banner Publishing:

"I dedicate this book to my wife, Sandy. She has continuously demonstrated faithfulness to God and her family through thirty-seven years of marriage. She has taught me the true biblical meaning of continuous knocking for the Lord. Without her love and faithfulness, I could not have written this book."

Now, let me show you the dedication in the book, *Rules for Radicals*, by Saul Alinsky. Remember, those who are serving the devil in the arena of politics are using this book as their playbook and guide.

"Lest we forget at least an over the shoulder acknowledgement to the very first radical: from all our legends, mythology and history, (and who is to know where mythology leaves off and history begins or which is which) the first radical known to man who rebelled against the establishment and did it so effectively that he at least won his own kingdom – Lucifer."

Saul Alinsky dedicated his book to Satan, a.k.a. Lucifer. Keep in mind that Alinsky is a hero to Barack Obama and Hillary Clinton. Obama moved to Chicago so he could be like his hero, Saul Alinsky, who was a community organizer in Chicago. Obama religiously taught from the book *Rules for Radicals* while he was a community organizer in Chicago working for ACORN. He unabashedly taught the tenets from the book, especially one of the primary principles extolling the virtues of the notion that the end justifies the means. Speaking lies and false accusations are not considered problems but as necessary tools to wrest freedoms from ordinary people. He taught straight from the book that declares that socialism must be instituted at any cost, and that there are plenty of "useful idiots" to do the heavy lifting so the ruling elite can enjoy the spoils of stolen property.

Hillary Clinton's topic for her thesis was the writings of Saul Alinsky. Hillary (then) Rodham wrote her thesis in 1969 in order to fulfill her requirements for a Bachelor of Arts degree from Wellesley College. The title of the ninety-two-page paper was "There is Only the Fight: An Analysis of the Alinsky Model." In this paper, Rodham heaps lavish praise upon Alinsky, the radical activist who was bent on the destruction of our society and our freedoms. She also corresponded with Alinsky in strangely adoring letters. Hillary Rodham Clinton has been a devoted and faithful Alinskyite since reading his first book, *Reveille for Radicals*.

In the chapters that follow, I will expose some of the rules for radicals presented by Alinsky. You will be amazed at some of the principles proclaimed. You will learn about other heinous ideas and organizations as we address the Fabian Society, Planned Parenthood, Cloward and Piven, Agenda 21, organizations funded by George Soros, and more.

We will not just wring our hands because our freedoms are under attack. I declare, in the name of Jesus, that we will believe the promises of God and come to the wonderful revelation that there has never been a nation like the United States of America, and there never will!

Oh! Pastor David, you say, you are such a homer. You can say that because you were born and raised in the United States. Really? Well, consider the following. Israel was formed by God because God loved man. God wanted all men to see, through Israel, what it would be like (blessings) if they were to follow him and have God living in their midst.

The rest of the nations, except the United States of America, were created because man wanted to reject God. Remember the tower of Babel in Genesis chapter 11? We are told how God resisted man's desire to be a god unto himself and therefore separated the people by language. New nations were established because man had rejected God.

> And they said, "Come, let us build ourselves a city, and a tower whose top is in the heavens; let us make a name for ourselves, lest we be scattered abroad over the face of the whole earth." But the LORD came down to see the city and the tower which the sons of men had built. And the LORD said, "Indeed the people are one and they all have one language, and this is what they begin to do; now nothing that they propose to do will be withheld from them. Come, let Us go down and there confuse their language, that they may not understand one another's speech." So the LORD scattered them abroad from there over the face of all the earth, and they ceased building the city. Therefore its name is called Babel, because there the LORD confused the language of all the earth; and from there the LORD scattered them abroad over the face of all the earth (GENESIS 11:4-9 NKJV)

God rejected man's ideas of a brave new world, a new world order, or an open society without borders. He still rejects that demonic way of thinking today when confronted with similar views as espoused by George Soros and other like-minded atheists bent on destroying man's freedoms. The devil does not want you free to pursue and fulfill your kingdom destiny. We will revisit this in more detail in later chapters.

All nations besides Israel and the U.S.A. were formed because man rejected God. Israel was formed because God loved man. The United States of America is totally unique because it is the only nation in the history of the world that was formed because man loved God. Don't think that God didn't notice that fact.

Our founders established this nation under the leading of the hand of God and, in essence, said to God, "We want to do it Your way. What would please You? We are here to serve You. That's why we came here and we want one nation under God." They went on to establish a civil government modeled after the spiritual government of the Kingdom of God.

Here is a quote from our first Chief Justice of the Supreme Court, John Jay:

> *"Providence has given to our people the choice of their rulers and it is the duty as well as the privilege and interest of our Christian Nation to select and prefer Christians for their rulers."* –John Jay

There is no mention of separation of church and state in the U.S. Constitution or the Bill of Rights. Our very first amendment included in the Bill of Rights established freedom of religion. It says "freedom of religion" not "freedom from religion." The first mention of separation of church and state was in a letter written by Thomas Jefferson concerning keeping the state from interfering with the church. That was the primary reason our founders wanted to form this new nation.

Here are some more quotes from our founders:

"The general principles on which the fathers achieved independence were...the general principles of Christianity." - John Adams

"It cannot be emphasized too strongly or too often that this great nation was founded not by religionist, but by Christians; not on religion, but on the Gospel of Jesus Christ. For that reason alone, people of other faiths have been afforded freedom of worship here. – Patrick Henry

"The highest glory of the American Revolution was this: it connected in one indissoluble bond the principles of civil government with the principles of Christianity." - John Quincy Adams

The principles that established the government of the United States of America were principles found in the Word of God. For example, the three co-equal branches of government (judicial, legislative and executive) were modeled from the book of Isaiah:

For the LORD *is our judge, the* LORD *is our lawgiver, the* LORD *is our king; he will save us* (ISAIAH 33:22).

The USA is the only nation established because its founders said to God, in essence and in unity, "We love you and we put you in charge." The government of the United States is founded upon liberty brought forth by the Spirit of God. Using faithful men, God fashioned a natural law within a natural government as a picture of his perfect law of liberty, the Word of God.

Knowing that not all men would accept him, in his mercy God gave us a government with checks and balances so that even unredeemed men could experience a taste of liberty on the earth. This was necessary for the United States to fulfill its godly assignments. This earthly government was a natural picture of the liberty we receive in Christ. When worked in conjunction with godly principles, it produces good works and the gospel is promoted with its good rewards. It helps us be blessed to be a blessing.

The foundation of our government in the United States is the Holy Spirit and the Word of God. During the founding era (1760-1805), the Bible was cited in 34 percent of notable quotations from our founding fathers. Did you know that all fifty-five signers of the Declaration of Independence believed in the Bible as the divine truth, believed in the God of Scripture, and his personal intervention in our lives? Did you know that fifty-two of the fifty-five signers were deeply committed Christians?[1]

Immediately after creating the Declaration of Independence, the Continental Congress formed the American Bible Society and voted to purchase and import 20,000 copies of Scripture for the people of this new nation. The primary reason public schools were established in our nation was so that all children would be able to read and learn the Bible, God's Word. So, I disagree with President Obama who says that this is no longer a Christian nation. I say that this is a Christian nation and we will fulfill our godly assignments with the help of God.

I have a vision for this nation. I see a person standing over a podium that has the official seal of the President of the United States. I can't see who it is, but I know that it is the president. I hear the president say, standing in the authority of the office, "Over the United States of America, Jesus is Lord."

Let's not give up because things don't look good. Let's speak what God wants and what we want in agreement with God. God doesn't speak what he has if he doesn't have want he wants. He speaks what he wants until what he has becomes what he wants. As we are made in his image, we should do the same thing.

I don't know about you, but even if, God forbid, our nation does go down, I am not going down without a fight, and neither should you.

CHAPTER ONE

GOD GAVE US CAPITALISM

"Our Constitution was made only for a moral and religious people. It is wholly inadequate to government of any other." -- John Adams

Was John Adams, our second president, completely right? For sure, all forms of government work best with moral and religious people. By religious, Adams meant people who have a desire to please God through obedience to Scriptures out of love and not those who perform ceremonies by rote through fear.

Even socialism, with its demonic origins, could work if everyone was just like Jesus. If everyone thought, talked and walked like Jesus at all times, there would be no problems, even in a socialist society. The truth is that nobody acts exactly like Jesus and very few live almost like Jesus and most people make decisions based on what pleases their flesh, not based on what pleases God. This is the world we live in.

If you read the entire message from Adams, which includes the excerpt above, you will understand the point he was trying to make. He was trying to warn the people of our new nation that liberty entails responsibility. The more liberty we have, the more responsibility we have toward others. Jesus tells us, "For unto whomsoever much is given, of him shall be much required" (Luke 12:48b).

One of the main responsibilities of so much liberty is not to use that liberty to take away liberties and freedom from others. Adams and many of our founders knew that the more people abused their freedom by treading on the freedom of others, the bigger the government would become as new laws must be passed to protect people's rights.

In other words, American citizens are supposed to practice self-government. That's the best way to preserve our republic. The best way to practice self-government is to be a moral and religious people. This is a biblical concept.

The principles that established the government of the United States of America were principles found in the Word of God. The Declaration of Independence, the Constitution, and the Bill of Rights reflect principles declared in the Bible. A biblically based form of government must give individuals a great deal of personal liberty with little government intervention. There is a role for government, but its role should be kept to a minimum, especially on a federal level. All government must be kept as close to the local level as possible. The more people refuse to consider other's freedoms, the broader government must become. The broader government becomes, the fewer freedoms we enjoy.

"Moreover if your brother sins against you, go and tell him his fault between you and him alone. If he hears

you, you have gained your brother. But if he will not hear, take with you one or two more, that 'by the mouth of two or three witnesses every word may be established.' And if he refuses to hear them, tell it to the church but if he refuses even to hear the church, let him be to you like a heathen and a tax collector." (Matthew 18:15-17 NKJV)

Both the Bible and the First, Second, Ninth, and Tenth Amendments embrace the importance of governing self and family as the first level of governance. The opposite of that, global governance, is an abomination to God as revealed in Genesis chapter 11 where we see God's reaction to the tower of Babel and man's attempt at global governance. God wants man to do what is right because he chooses to, not because he is compelled to by fear.

> *"There is therefore now no condemnation to those who are in Christ Jesus, who do not walk according to the flesh, but according to the Spirit."* (ROMANS 8:1 NKJV)

God wants man to treat others as he would want to be treated.

> *"So in everything, do to others what you would have them do to you, for this sums up the Law and the Prophets."* (MATTHEW 7:12 NIV)

As alluded to previously, most men will not practice what has become known as "the golden rule" as stated in Mathew 7:12. We live in a world where there is a devil loose and where men cater to their flesh above all else. Bad decisions are made on a regular basis, and even good people can come into contact with the results of those bad decisions, even if they were made by others.

> *"In the world ye shall have tribulation: but be of good cheer; I have overcome the world."* (JOHN 16:33B)

God Almighty is not unaware of the world we live in. He is not caught off guard by men's sins. Sin is not God's will, but he will allow sin because he gave to man a free will. God was well aware of the devastating consequences of Adam's sin in the garden. God was not caught napping. God did not slap the fruit out of Adam's hand, because he had given Adam a free will. That freedom carried a great responsibility, which is now given to the church because the blood of Jesus has put us back in that place of freedom and responsibility.

> *"And God said, Let us make man in our image, after our likeness: and let them have dominion over the fish of the sea, and over the fowl of the air, and over the cattle, and over all the earth, and over every creeping thing that creepeth upon the earth. So God created man in his own image, in the image of God created he him; male and female created he them. And God blessed them, and God said unto them, Be fruitful, and multiply, and replenish the earth, and subdue it: and have dominion over the fish of the sea, and over the fowl of the air, and over every living thing that moveth upon the earth."* (GENESIS 1:26-28)

Don't blame God for the mess we are in. He said let *us* make man, but let *them* have dominion. Remember, with great freedom comes great responsibility to carry out an assignment for God. We will examine in greater detail our freedom/liberty and thus our dominion mandate in a later chapter.

> "For if by the one man's offense death reigned through the one, much more those who receive abundance of grace and of the gift of righteousness will reign in life through the One, Jesus Christ." (Romans 5:17 NKJV)

> "If the Son therefore shall make you free, ye shall be free indeed." (John 8:36)

> "For this is the will of God, that by doing good you may put to silence the ignorance of foolish men—as free, yet not using liberty as a cloak for vice, but as bondservants of God." (1 Peter 2:15-16 NKJV)

God gave dominion on earth to his people and not to himself. He knows that men won't always do right. He wants us to choose to obey him out of love. You always do a better job in any task when you do it because you *want* to than when you do it because you *have* to. Nothing happens that God does not already know about in advance. God is not limited to time and space. For more on this subject, see my book *Inhabiting Eternity on Earth*.

> "Remember the former things of old, For I am God, and there is no other; I am God, and there is none like Me, Declaring the end from the beginning, And from ancient times things that are not yet done, Saying, 'My counsel shall stand, And I will do all My pleasure,'" (Isaiah 46:9-10 NKJV)

God knows what is going to happen and he also knows that without Jesus, a man's heart is wicked. Man cannot see into another man's heart, but God can.

> "The heart is deceitful above all things, and desperately

wicked: who can know it?" (JEREMIAH 17:9 NKJV)

Thank God that because of Jesus we can serve others and love our fellow man as well as loving God.

"I will give them an undivided heart and put a new spirit in them; I will remove from them their heart of stone and give them a heart of flesh. Then they will follow my decrees and be careful to keep my laws. They will be my people, and I will be their God." (EZEKIEL 11:19-20 NIV)

Our founding fathers loved Jesus. Even though they were brilliant men, they knew that only God could come up with a form of government that could work for those who sought to please God and for all other men as well. What did they do? They sought the face of God and let God lead them to put together a government for a country where men could be free to honor and obey God.

They probably did not fully realize the plan and the godly assignments waiting for our great nation. They simply followed and obeyed God, and the result was the greatest nation in the history of the world. Because of God's great love for man, God gave our founders, through revelation by the Spirit of God, the American free-enterprise capitalistic system. God loves people so much he gave us a government that blesses our nation, even though it contains lots of selfish people!

Pastor David, you say, can you back that up? Yes, I can. Keep reading and read with an open mind. As discussed earlier, God knew that the world, and thus our nation, would be full of people pursuing their separate interests with more regard for their own happiness than for the happiness of others. The Declaration of Independence refers to this as the "pursuit of happiness." It also states that the pursuit of happiness is an inalienable right given to us by our Creator along with the rights of life and liberty.

Why is it so hard to understand that the pursuit of happiness is just as much from God as is life and liberty? Our founders were very wise and had a lot of spiritual discernment. They understood this concept, at least in part. Capitalism, in its truest form, trains people to want to do right and to serve others as they follow their dreams. In such a society, even the lost man can live in peace with his neighbor without violating the rights of others.

A good capitalist has happy customers and happy employees. He has to serve his customers with products or services that they want or need at a fair price. He learns that serving others is good for him, his family, his customers, his community, and the nation. He learns that he can't serve his customers to the full without happy, pleasant, well-trained employees. He learns to realize the biblical (even though he may not know it's biblical) principle of being a servant-leader.

As he endeavors to work capitalism, even for his own self interest, he sees demonstrated before his eyes the principles of the kingdom of God that the founders wanted for this nation. He learns through observation and then in practice that customers value, and are loyal to, businesses that are involved in and help the local community. His giving causes his business to prosper and he is more able to bless his valuable employees. They, in turn, can bless their families and other businesses as their standard of living is increased.

When the capitalist sees the fruit from his giving in the community, he feels so good about it that he wants to do more. He realizes that the more he gives the more business comes to him from the community. Therefore, he can increase his giving and not be diminished, but rather, increased.

Now, the capitalist is really learning about the kingdom. Without setting foot in a church, he can learn more about how the kingdom of God works than some preachers I know. Through the American free-enterprise capitalistic system, he is trained to do right because he wants to, not because he has to. That is the way God wants his children to live. That's the kingdom way. God wants us to learn to treat others the way we want to be treated, even in a sinful world. So he gave us capitalism.

When things are not profitable, a capitalist must make some adjustments if he wants his business, which he has invested so much in, to continue. The loss part of a profit-and-loss system is important. With consistent losses, the capitalist must regroup and find ways to either provide a better product or service for the same price, or become more efficient to offer the same product at a lower price. Either way, the customer is better served. If not, someone else will come along to serve them better. Capitalism is all about serving others, even when the capitalist's motive is to pursue his own self interest.

A capitalistic society creates the best environment for people to hear the Gospel and be saved and for the believer to seek to fulfil his kingdom destiny. The higher the standard of living, the more men are at peace. A man is more inclined to peacefully reflect on and talk about spiritual things when he is not consumed with how he is going to feed his children. God wants men to live in peace.

> *"I urge, then, first of all, that petitions, prayers, intercession and thanksgiving be made for all people— for kings and all those in authority, that we may live peaceful and quiet lives in all godliness and holiness. This is good, and pleases God our Savior, who wants all people to be saved and to come to a knowledge of the truth."* (1 Timothy 2:1-4 NIV)

With a high standard of living gained through capitalism, people can receive the good news about the goodness of God more easily than they can when they are starving and without hope, which is what socialism brings. The Bible says that it is the goodness of God that leads to repentance, and repentance leads to salvation.

God wants us to have more than enough because he wants the best for his children, and he wants the lost to become his children. These are only some of the reasons he gave us capitalism. Why were the people of the United States so special that he only gave it to us? The answer is that we are not more special than anyone else. Everything that God has is for whosoever will. Our nation had the only founders who actually listened to God and then obeyed. Any nation can have the same if they will do the same.

Later in this book, we will see in great detail that socialism is evil. The devil wants capitalism gone so people won't have the freedom to choose God and the freedom to choose to obey him. God wants his people blessed so that we can be a blessing.

"Socialism is a philosophy of failure, the creed of ignorance, and the gospel of envy. Its inherent virtue is the equal sharing of misery." -- Winston Churchill

"The problem with socialism is that you eventually run out of other people's money." -- Margaret Thatcher

"No one would remember the Good Samaritan if he'd only had good intentions; he had money as well." -- Margaret Thatcher

CHAPTER TWO

THE ORIGIN OF MODERN SOCIALISM

Modern socialism has an element of stealth and secrecy to it. I am defining modern socialism as starting with the Fabian Society in 1884. Prior to the Fabians, there were plenty of tyrants and dictators who controlled other's lives, but real socialism began with the writings of Karl Marx. He was not secretive about what he believed. There was no strategy of stealth.

In 1848, Marx published *The Communist Manifesto* along with Freidrich Engels. In 1867, he published the first volume of *Das Kapital*. Marx died in 1883. Marx never earned a living wage and was largely supported by Engels. No wonder he liked socialism!

Unlike Marx, who stated exactly what he wanted to happen, the Fabian socialists were full of deception. This deception was the origin and became the key element, the mainstay and foundation of modern socialism. In 1884, the Fabian Society began its quest of a new world order through stamina and guile.

The Fabian Society is a British socialist organization, formed for the purpose of advancing the principles of socialism by slow, deceitful methods rather than by sudden overthrow. The Fabian Society founded the London School of Economics. It also founded the Labour Party in 1900, which still has influence in modern British politics as evidenced by the election of Tony Blair as Prime Minister, who served in that capacity from 1997 to 2007.

"Whereas communists wanted to establish socialism quickly through violence and revolution, the Fabians preferred to do it slowly through propaganda and legislation. The word socialism was not to be used. Instead, they would speak of benefits for the people such as welfare, medical care, higher wages and better working conditions."[2]

In its early stages, the Fabians included many prestigious, propaganda-styled writers including George Bernard Shaw, H.G. Wells, Aldous Huxley, Jack London and Virginia Woolf. The Society had two very public and prominent members who were the faces of the organization as well as its ad hoc designated spokesmen. These two men were George Bernard Shaw and H.G. Wells. Just as Alinsky dedicated his book to Lucifer, the Fabian socialists had clandestine intentions that they referred to as the "Luciferian goal."

This is how it was stated by playwright George Bernard Shaw: "Under socialism, you would not be allowed to be poor. You would be forcibly fed, clothed, lodged, taught, and employed whether you liked it or not. If it were discovered that you had not character and industry enough to be worth all this trouble, you might possibly be executed in a kindly manner; but whilst you were permitted to live, you would have to live well."

The Fabians knew that if they were open and honest about their intentions from the start, they could not win. They were aware that Marx was expelled from Germany and France as a result of his socialistic writings. The Fabian method was to do things gradually using deception. Their method was similar to putting a frog in a pot of water and gradually turning up the heat until the frog is dead.

The Fabian Society was named in honor of the Roman General Fabius Maximus, who was nicknamed The Delayer. The strategy of Fabius Maximus was gradual victory through persistence, harassment, and wearing down the enemy by attrition rather than by head on battles.[3] He adopted this strategy, which proved to be successful, in order to defeat the more able and stronger Carthaginian army under the renowned General Hannibal. This became the model of operation for the Fabian Society.

The Fabian Society's first pamphlet stated the following: "For the right moment you must wait, as Fabius did most patiently, when warring against Hannibal, though many censured his delays; but when the time comes you must strike hard, as Fabius did, or your waiting will be in vain, and fruitless." This notion can be stated more succinctly and in modern words as spoken by Rahm Emanuel, President Obama's first chief of staff, "never let a good crisis go to waste."

The logo of the Fabian Society is an angry tortoise with the words "when I strike, I strike hard" written below the tortoise. Its coat of arms (later dropped as people realized its significance) was a picture of a wolf in sheep's clothing. This coincides with its philosophy to deceive people as to their motivations until it is too late.

"Watch out for false prophets. They come to you in sheep's clothing, but inwardly they are ferocious wolves. By their fruit you will recognize them. Do people pick grapes from thorn bushes, or figs from thistles? Likewise, every good tree bears good fruit, but a bad tree bears bad fruit. A good tree cannot bear bad fruit, and a bad tree cannot bear good fruit. Every tree that does not bear good fruit is cut down and thrown into the fire. Thus, by their fruit you will recognize them." (MATTHEW 7:15-20 NIV)

Jesus did not adhere to the philosophy of the Fabians, Saul Alinsky, Hillary Clinton or Barack Obama, which is the end justifies the means. He knew that the end (or tree) was bad if the means (the fruit) was bad. Besides that, the end the Fabians were seeking, which was the loss of liberties for the masses, is also bad and originates from Satan. It truly is a Luciferian goal.

Many people are familiar with the works of author H. G. Wells. They know about *The Invisible Man, The Time Machine, War of the Worlds,* and *The Island of Dr. Moreau.* What you might not be familiar with is *A Modern Utopia, The Shape of Things to Come,* and *The Open Conspiracy.* The latter book details how Fabians and other like-minded socialists could bypass the existing mechanisms of governments and the will of the people and implement their agenda gradually.

Aldous Huxley penned the novel *Brave New World* about a world in which the state controls the lives of the common people. Huxley pitches that the ruling elite would take such good care of the masses in such a society. It's for the good of the collective, don't you see? This notion is demonic and goes against the way of the Kingdom of God. All good things from God are for whosoever will. It's God's desire for no one to be deceived, that we would all know the truth, and be free to pursue our own destiny.

"Then you will know the truth, and the truth will set you free." (JOHN 8:32 NIV)

Huxley was the mentor of the young George Orwell (real name Eric Blair) who eventually saw through the hoax of the Fabians and totally rejected their teachings and philosophy. This caused him to write *Animal Farm* in 1945 and *1984* in 1949 so that he could fight fire with fire. He used literature, particularly novels, to expose the lies and reveal the dangers of socialism. Orwell chose 1984 because that marked 100 years after the establishment of the Fabian Society. Orwell was demonstrating that the Fabians were willing to wait 100 years, if necessary, and gave us a glimpse of what the world would be like if they fully succeeded. It would be a world beyond repair.

"No one ever seizes power with the intention of relinquishing it. Power is not a means it is an end."
- George Orwell

"All animals are equal, but some are more equal than others." - *George Orwell in Animal Farm*

"Big Brother is watching you." - *George Orwell in 1984*

The Fabian Society created a stained glass window as a statement of intent. It was commissioned by George Bernard Shaw and was displayed in the home of Sidney and Beatrice Webb, two of the original founders. The window shows Shaw and Sidney Webb standing over a melting fire, hammering the world into their chosen shape. At the top of the window are the words "REMOULD IT NEARER TO THE HEART'S DESIRE."

At the bottom is H.G. Wells thumbing his nose at Lenin's "useful idiots" worshipping books that extol the virtues of socialism. The wolf in sheep's clothing emblem points to the molten world being reshaped by those with total disregard for human life and liberty.

The world is melted down because to get where they want to go, the world must first be destroyed and brought to naught so they could start over. What the socialist wanted then, and now, is to be the god of your life because they know what is best for you better than you do. When you have time, search the web for the image of the Fabian window and the Fabian motto and the Fabian coat of arms. The Fabian notion of destroying freedoms to remold the world to a socialist elitist heart's desire is alive today.

"We are at a stage in history in which remolding society is one of the greatest challenges facing all of us in the West." - Hillary Clinton

The heart's desire stated on the window is articulated by H. G. Wells. "It is outright world socialism, scientifically planned and directed."

This is merely an updated version of the tower of Babel. It's just man trying to be God and exert power over others. God said we have dominion over animals that walk the earth, birds that fly, fish that swim, and seed-bearing plants. We do not have dominion over other people made in the image of God.

Socialism is presented as something that is good for everyone. It operates as Satan does, masquerading as an angel of light. Socialists always profess "good" intentions for their use of force, coercion, and intimidation upon mankind. Socialism philosophy uses lies, deceit, and gradually kills, steals, and destroys.

"The thief cometh not, but for to steal, and to kill, and to destroy: I am come that they might have life, and that they might have it more abundantly." (JOHN 10:10)

"You belong to your father, the devil, and you want to carry out your father's desires. He was a murderer from the beginning, not holding to the truth, for there is no truth in him. When he lies, he speaks his native language, for he is a liar and the father of lies." (JOHN 8:44 NIV)

In the early 1900s, the Fabian Society members advocated the idea of a scientifically planned society and supported eugenics by sterilization. Their goal was to rid the world of "undesirables." People who didn't live up to their standards had to be eliminated one way or another.

This philosophy of eugenics manifested in the United States in large part through H.G. Wells' lover, Margaret Sanger, the founder of The American Birth Control League, which later became known as Planned Parenthood. Her stated goal and vision was to use sterilization to eliminate black people and other undesirables, such as the mentally challenged, from the earth. If sterilization didn't stop black children from being conceived, then the next step was to kill them in the womb. Even today, when Planned Parenthood makes selections for new locations, they select locations centered within large black populations. Hillary Clinton has stated numerous times how she admires the vision of Margaret Sanger. The Nazi Party leaders acknowledged that they got the idea of sterilization from Margaret Sanger. We will learn more about Planned Parenthood in a later chapter.

The real goal of socialism is to create a small ruling elite to exercise power over the masses. The elites want to make decisions for the rest of us because, in their minds, we can't make good decisions. In their demonic thinking, the inability of the masses to make decisions that the elites would agree with justifies the seizing of property, freedoms, and even life from the masses.

Here is a quote from George Bernard Shaw that discloses how he feels he would treat people properly, because he would tell them they have to die, but he would do it in a kind manner:

> *"You must all know a half a dozen people, at least, who are no use in this world, who are more trouble than they are worth. Just put them there and say, Sir or Madam, will you be kind enough to justify your existence. If you can't justify your existence, if you're not pulling your weight in your social group, if you are not producing as much as you consume or perhaps a little more, then, clearly, we cannot use the big organization of our society for the purpose of keeping you alive because your life does not benefit us and it can't be of very much use to yourself." - George Bernard Shaw*

The above words are horrific and bone chilling. When you pull back the curtain of an elitist socialist, this is what you find. I'm not talking about the deceived common folk who are merely Kool-Aid drinkers who don't realize the poison they are drinking. The Nazi Party (National Socialist Party) not only learned sterilization from the Fabians and Sanger, but they also learned about mass killings from the semi-secret society. Here is what Shaw proclaimed:

> "I appeal to the chemists to discover a humane gas that will kill instantly and painlessly. Deadly by all means, but humane, not cruel." - George Bernard Shaw

Ten years later, the Nazi killing machine came up with such a gas. It was called Zyklon B. Adolf Eichmann, the man who supervised the administration of the gas to the Jews, gave this testimony about Zyklon B and talked about a humane gas using the very same words as Shaw:

> "Thanks to Zyklon B, the people of Auschwitz died without pain. Zyklon B was a humane gas." - Adolf Eichmann

The Fabians were for mass killings, yet they thought Hitler's slaughter wasn't up to their standards. According to Fabians, you kill by class and not by nationality or religion, and certainly not any productive people. Rather, you kill the idle and the infirm. The reason socialism has had such a long hard climb in the U.S.A. is because of our U.S. Constitution. It is what protects us from foreign monsters and from monsters from within. We must hold fast to it as it was given to us by God as a blessing and for our protection.

Shaw complained about our Constitution because it kept him from making inroads in our country. Our Constitution is a hedge of protection in the natural. The devil complains about a spiritual hedge and Shaw complains about a natural hedge. Shaw lectured the people of our nation in the following quote:

> *"I told you in New York. I put it to you very carefully and exactly. I told you what you had to do in this country was to abolish your constitution which is preventing you from doing anything. And now you see what's happened since. Every attempt you made to do anything, the Supreme Court immediately stops it saying it's against the Constitution. Well, I tell you again, get rid of your Constitution."* - George Bernard Shaw

> *"Have you not put a hedge around him and his household and everything he has? You have blessed the work of his hands, so that his flocks and herds are spread throughout the land."* (JOB 1:10 NIV)

God's people praying (spiritual) and the Constitution (natural) have largely kept socialism from overtaking our nation. God loves all people. Therefore, he gave us the Constitution so that even the lost man could have a chance at a good life. Remember, God loves all people, and his ways of a civil government are available to all nations. But no other nation would listen to him.

The socialists are still working the slow way, waiting for a chance to strike and strike hard when opportunity arises. They would like for you to justify your life like Shaw suggested, but they will start smaller and work their way up to your life. First, they want you to justify your guns. It's one step at a time. Besides, they can't take your life until they first take away your guns. New Jersey and New York City now have gun laws where you have to justify why you need a gun. A right enumerated in the Bill of Rights does not need to be justified.

In New York City, you won't get a carry permit without showing cause. With your application you must include a Letter of Necessity justifying your need for a gun. The New Jersey application reads as follows "Every applicant not applying as a law enforcement officer must demonstrate justifiable need in order to obtain a permit, by means of a letter detailing specific need attached to the justification."

In London, where the Fabians began, they had no hedge of protection of the U.S. Constitution. Sadly, in the country where the Magna Carta was signed, parts of the city of London have become sharia law zones where London police ("bobbies") are not allowed. It's worse than bringing a knife to a gun fight. All they've got to bring is a stick! In those areas, women, homosexuals, Christians, and many others have very few rights. London has just elected its first Muslim mayor.

We must fight to keep the freedoms given to us by God. It is a spiritual battle and a natural battle. We can't let our guard down, because just like the angry tortoise of the Fabians, socialist elites are waiting patiently for us to let our guard down. They are in it for the long haul. This is what Nikita Khrushchev, former premier of the Soviet Union, spoke to Ezra Benson, then Secretary of Agriculture of the U.S. under President Eisenhower:

> *"You Americans are so gullible. No, you won't accept communism outright, but we'll keep feeding you small doses of socialism until you'll finally wake up and find you already have communism. We won't have to fight you. We'll so weaken your economy until you'll fall like overripe fruit into our hands."* - Nikita Khrushchev

Hillary Clinton also thinks that Democrat voters are useful idiots to be used and manipulated. Dick Morris, a close confidant to Hillary Clinton, recorded the following about Ms. Clinton in his book *Rewriting History*:

> *"Hillary knows full well who she is and what parts of her must never be exposed to public view... Her trickery is designed to hide her most basic character and instincts from all of us... We only see what she wants us to see."*

The good news is that we already have what we need to defeat socialism. We have the Spirit of God in us, we have the Word of God, and in the natural we have the Constitution. We should proclaim our freedom knowing we have the authority over the enemy and his attempts to control people. Socialists are like Lucifer. They want to control people. They want to be like a god, and that is evil.

> *"How you are fallen from heaven, O Lucifer son of the morning! How you are cut down to the ground, You who weakened the nations! For you have said in your heart: 'I will ascend into heaven, I will exalt my throne above the stars of God; I will also sit on the mount of the congregation On the farthest sides of the north; I will ascend above the heights of the*

clouds, I will be like the Most High.'" (ISAIAH 14:12-14 NKJV)

What happened in the Kingdom of Heaven to a socialist elitist? What happened to someone who wanted to be like God with power to control others? He was cast out. What do we do on earth as citizens of heaven? We cast them out. How? We cast our ballot for a freedom-loving capitalist candidate, and the socialists or the democratic socialists will be cast out.

CHAPTER THREE

LEARNING FROM HISTORY

Why couldn't socialism work? It can't work because Satan is its architect. Don't take my word for it. Let's look at history. Socialism has failed 100 percent of the time. Those talking about the collective and a new world order and a world without borders are not coming up with anything new. It has been tried many times, as far back as the tower of Babel, and failed every time. To find out what is happening today you can always look at history.

> *"What has been will be again, what has been done will be done again; there is nothing new under the sun. Is there anything of which one can say, `Look! This is something new`? It was here already, long ago; it was here before our time."* (ECCLESIASTES 1:9-10 NIV)

> *"That which is has already been, And what is to be has already been; And God requires an account of what is past."* (ECCLESIASTES 3:15 NKJV)

After 240 years as a democratic republic, this nation is in jeopardy. Approximately 40 percent to 50 percent of the nation's population has already reached the government dependency stage. Below is a quote largely attributed to Alexander Tytler, a Scottish history professor at the University of Edinburg in 1787 addressing the fall of the Athenian Republic:

"A democracy will continue to exist up until the time that voters discover that they can vote themselves generous gifts from the public treasury. From that moment on, the majority always votes for the candidates who promise the most benefits from the public treasury, with the result that every democracy will finally collapse over loose fiscal policy, which is always followed by a dictatorship.

The average age of the world's greatest civilizations from the beginning of history has been about 200 years. During those 200 years, these nations always progressed through the following sequence:

From bondage to spiritual faith;

From spiritual faith to great courage;

From courage to liberty;

From liberty to abundance;

From abundance to complacency;

From complacency to apathy;

From apathy to dependence;

From dependence back into bondage."

The United States election in November 2016 is of vital importance. If we grant amnesty and citizenship to 12 to 20 million (estimated) illegal aliens, then we might lose this nation forever. When socialism gets entrenched in a nation, it is always followed by dictatorship, and then very bad things happen.

In the twentieth century, it is estimated that from 50 to 70 million people were victims of mass murders perpetrated by governments with dictators where socialism prevailed. They accomplish these heinous crimes after confiscating virtually all guns from their populations.

In 1929, the Soviet Union established gun control. Private gun ownership was totally abolished under Joseph Stalin. From 1929 to 1953 in the Soviet Union, about 20 million dissidents, unable to defend themselves, were exterminated under the orders of Joseph Stalin. The following are quotes of Stalin:

> "Ideas are more powerful than guns. We would not let our enemies have guns, why would we let them have ideas."
>
> "Death is a solution to all problems. No man – no problem."
>
> "The death of one man is a tragedy. The death of millions is a statistic."
>
> "God is on your side? Is he a conservative? The devil is on my side, he's a good communist."

Solomon, the wisest man who ever lived, answers the

above question from Stalin:

> "*The heart of the wise inclines to the right, but the heart of a fool to the left.*" (ECCLESIASTES 10:2 NIV)

In 1911, Turkey established full gun control. From 1915 to 1917, over 1.5 million out of the 2.5 million Armenians, unable to defend themselves, were exterminated.

In March of 1938, Hitler, still called Chancellor, but in reality a dictator, directed the Nazis to create their own weapons law. On November 9, 1938, the Nazis launched Kristallnacht, also known as The Night of Broken Glass. The government disarmed Jews and released government-sponsored mobs which destroyed 250 synagogues. In addition, over seven thousand Jewish shops were ransacked and looted and thirty thousand Jews were removed to concentration camps. An official SS report claimed ninety-one dead as a result of the assaults on Jews.

Joseph Goebbels, Nazi minister of propaganda, and Reinhard Heydrich, second in command of the SS after Heinrich Himmler, ordered the attacks with a prior notice to police to not interfere. The official line of the Nazis was that the attacks were a result of "spontaneous demonstrations" against Jews. The Nazi propaganda minister was so arrogant that he tried to sell an impossible-to-believe lie that the deaths and destruction were unplanned, as they were spontaneous demonstrations. The devil never changes his tactics. Hillary Clinton and Barack Obama tried to sell an impossible-to-believe lie that the deaths and destruction in Benghazi were from a "spontaneous demonstration" over a video.

In conjunction with Kristallnacht, the German government used the authority of the 1938 Weapons Law to require Jewish surrender of all firearms and edged weapons and to mandate a sentence of death or twenty years in a concentration camp for any violation. From 1939 to 1945, 11 million Jews and others (about 6 million Jews), unable to defend themselves, were exterminated.

"Germans who wish to use firearms should join the SS or the SA, ordinary citizens don't need guns, as their having guns doesn't serve the state." - Heinrich Himmler

In 1935, China established gun control. From 1949 to 1952, 20 million political dissidents, unable to defend themselves, were exterminated by Mao Zedong. Still with no guns for the masses, Mao Zedong's Chinese Cultural Revolution from 1966 to 1976 "claimed the lives of several million people and afflicted cruel and inhuman treatments on hundreds of million people" says Mass Violence.org. "However, 40 years after it ended, the total number of victims of the Cultural Revolution and especially the death toll of mass killings still remain a mystery both in China and overseas."[4]

"All political power comes from the barrel of a gun. The communist party must command all the guns, that way, no guns can ever be used to command the party." – Mao Zedong

In 1964, Guatemala established gun control. From 1964 to 1981, one hundred thousand Mayan Indians, unable to defend themselves, were exterminated. In 1970, Uganda established gun control. From 1971 to 1979, three hundred thousand people, unable to defend themselves, were rounded up and exterminated. In 1956, Cambodia established gun control. From 1975 to 1977, over 1 million people, unable to defend themselves, were exterminated.

> *"When a strong man, fully armed, guards his own house, his possessions are safe. But when someone stronger attacks and overpowers him, he takes away the armor in which the man trusted and divides up his plunder."* (LUKE 11:21-22 NIV)

Perhaps all of these executions would have happened anyway, but probably not. I can say for sure that it would have been more difficult to execute so many victims if they had had guns to defend themselves, and the vast majority of these victims, were indeed, defenseless.

That is why the restrictions on and confiscation of guns is so important to tyrants who want to take away our freedoms. These men and women are the epitome of wolves in sheep's clothing. Hillary Clinton touts that gun control would make the streets safer. Tell that to the victims of The Night of Broken Glass and the millions of Jews tossed into the gas chambers.

> *"We've got to rein in what has become almost an article of faith that almost anybody can have a gun anywhere at any time." - Hillary Clinton*

There are good reasons that the Second Amendment to the Constitution declares the following: "The Right of the people to keep and bear arms shall not be infringed."

There has never been a communist nation or a mostly socialist nation or a nation with a dictator where gun ownership among the civilian population is a cherished right. I wonder why? Below is what Senator Barack Obama said in July 2008 revealing his highest hopes for the "hope and change" he dreamed of bringing to our country:

> "We cannot continue to rely on our military in order to achieve the national security objectives we have set. We've got to have a civilian national security force that's just as powerful, just as strong, just as well funded." –Barack Obama

This sounds just like the East German Secret Police. To my knowledge, no one in a free country has ever proposed such a massive national police force.

Hitler, Himmler, Lenin, Stalin, Zedong and Amin espoused gun control. Our founding fathers were relentless in declaring the right to bear arms. Who do you think had more wisdom from God, a bunch of murdering butchers or the founders of the greatest nation in the history of the world? Here are some quotes from our founders concerning an armed civilian population.

> "When governments fear the people, there is liberty. When the people fear the government, there is tyranny. No free man shall ever be debarred the use of arms. The strongest reason for the people to retain the right to keep and bear arms is, as a last resort, to protect themselves against tyranny in government." - Thomas Jefferson

> "Guard with jealous attention the public liberty. Suspect every one who approaches that jewel. Unfortu-

nately, nothing will preserve it but downright force. Whenever you give up force, you are ruined...The great object is that every man be armed." – Patrick Henry

"The best we can hope for concerning the people at large is that they be properly armed." – Alexander Hamilton

"The Constitution shall never be construed to authorize Congress to prevent the people of the United States, who are peaceable citizens, from keeping their own arms." – Samuel Adams

"Americans need never fear their government because the advantage of being armed, which Americans possess over the people of almost every other nation." – James Madison

"Firearms stand next in importance to the Constitution itself. They are the American people's liberty teeth and keystone under independence...The very atmosphere of firearms everywhere restrains evil interference. They deserve a place of honor with all that's good." –George Washington

Socialism unchecked always brings total tyranny subsequent to gun control, and has nothing good to offer. The importance of the right to bear arms will be even more magnified in the chapter discussing the U. N. plan through Agenda 21. Nothing good comes out of socialism – not ever. Socialism fails and brings heartache, sorrow, poverty, fear, and even death 100 percent of the time. Not 99 percent, not 99.9 percent, not 99.9999 percent, but every single time without exception all throughout history.

Below is an interesting transcript from a 1979 episode of the Phil Donahue Show. Donahue interviews the late, great Milton Friedman, a great advocate for capitalism. It is a reminder that there is nothing new under the sun.

Donahue: "When you see around the globe the mal distribution of wealth, the desperate plight of millions of people in under developed countries, when you see so few haves and so many have-nots, when you see the greed and the concentration of power, did you ever have a moment of doubt about capitalism and whether greed is a good idea to run on?"

Friedman: "Tell me, is there some society you know that doesn't run on greed? Do you think Russia doesn't run on greed? Do you think China doesn't run on greed? The world runs on individuals pursuing their separate interests. The greatest achievements of civilization have not come from government bureaus. Einstein did not construct his theory under orders from a bureaucrat. Henry Ford did not revolutionize the automobile industry that way. In the only cases in which the masses have escaped from the kind of grinding poverty you are talking about, is where they have had capitalism and largely free trade. If you want to know where the masses are worse off, it's exactly in the kinds of societies that depart from that.

The record of history is absolutely crystal clear. There is no alternative way, so far discovered, of improving the lot of ordinary people that can hold a candle to the productive activities that are unleashed by free enterprise systems."

Donahue: "But it seems to reward, not virtue, as much as the ability to manipulate the system."

Friedman: "And what does reward virtue? Do you think the communist Commissar rewards virtue? Do you think a Hitler rewards virtue? Do you think, excuse me, that American presidents reward virtue? Do they choose their appointees on the basis of the virtue of the people appointed or on the basis of their political clout? Is it really true that political self-interest is nobler somehow than economic self-interest?

You know, I think you are taking a lot of things for granted. Just tell me where in the world do you find these angels who are going to organize our society for us? I don't even trust you to do that."

I am not saying that God wants us to have greed. The way of greed and envy is the way of the world and the devil. What I have declared in chapter 1 is that God knew that not every man would follow him whole-heartedly. Through his kindness and wisdom, and because of the obedient hearts of our founders, he gave us a system of government to bless our nation so that we can fulfill this nation's godly assignments. For more on the role of envy in socialism and the kingdom of darkness, and the role of reward motivation in capitalism and the kingdom of God, see my book *Was Jesus a Socialist or a Capitalist?*

Let's take a moment to think about how God pursues his own self-interest and that he does it by loving people and serving people. It should be the same for us. Capitalism trains us to live like God. We pursue our dreams from God, which we believe by faith are in our self-interest.

We reap the rewards generated by following the kingdom principles of loving, giving, and serving, because we trust God to be faithful to his promises. God sees our faith and is pleased. That's why he created us. It was for his pleasure as he experiences our love and trust.

> *"Thou art worthy, O Lord, to receive glory and honour and power: for thou hast created all things, and for thy pleasure they are and were created."* (REVELATION 4:11)

> *"And so we know and rely on the love God has for us. God is love. Whoever lives in love lives in God, and God in them." (1 JOHN 4:16 NIV)*

> *"But he that is greatest among you shall be your servant." (MATTHEW 23:11)*

> *"And without faith it is impossible to please God, because anyone who comes to him must believe that he exists and that he rewards those who earnestly seek him." (HEBREWS 11:6 NIV)*

God is pleased when we believe him. Belief in the promises of God causes us to obey God, and serve and love others. We know that as we serve others and give to others, we are not diminished but blessed and increased. Without faith in the promises of God, we would not obey.

In other words, it takes faith to live like God and faith is what pleases God. If we were made to please God, then we were made to live like God by pursuing our dreams through loving, serving, and blessing others just like our heavenly Father, because we were made by him to be in his image.

If we want to live like God we must think like God. When we think like God we will talk like God. When we talk like God we will walk like God. When we walk like God we will live like God on this earth. We will make it on earth as it is in heaven. For more revelation about thinking and living like God on earth, please see my book *The Goodness of God.*

Let's look at history found in the Bible. Following Joseph's rise to prominence in Egypt, God's people in Egypt lived according to the way the Lord directed them. Government for his people was set up to function by the design of God. As a result, the people of Israel had the very best in all the land in Egypt. They were far from the ways of socialism. They trusted in their God, the one true God.

As a result, they had more than enough to freely help others. Helping others would be a decision that they could make of their own free will, not by edict of the government. In Egypt, Pharaoh may have promoted the notion of how great government assistance can be. However, the people of Egypt did not survive their food shortage crisis because of Pharaoh or the government of Egypt. The people made it through the crisis because of Joseph. Egypt was not blessed because of its greatness. No, the people were rescued and had provision because of Joseph's relationship with God Almighty. The people of the U.S. have not been blessed because of our good works, but because of our founders' relationship with God Almighty.

God showed Joseph how to deal with governing the people of Egypt and God showed our founders how to deal with the governance of the people of our new nation.

The people of Egypt benefited from the faith, virtues, and principles that Joseph displayed. They received this benefit because it rains on the just and the unjust. The ungodly people living in the U.S.A. today are benefiting from the faith, virtues, and principles our founders displayed.

Even with a decline in the acceptance of the greatness of the United States today, it is still, by far, the most blessed nation in the world. This nation is blessed, not because of atheists, socialists, communists, Marxists, Muslims, and other folks who disrespect or hate the God of Abraham, Isaac, and Jacob. It is blessed because of God's people who desire to please him and operate according to the principles of the kingdom of God.

Because of God's people, we are the most giving, most generous nation in the history of the world. The people of our nation also have the highest standard of living in the world because it rains on the just and the unjust. The communists, socialists, and the rest of the folks outside of church of the Lord Jesus Christ get the benefit of great provision, opportunity, freedom, and liberty because of God's people.

"Now the Lord is that Spirit: and where the Spirit of the Lord is, there is liberty." (2 CORINTHIANS 3:17).

The Hebrews had freedom and liberty to lead their lives as they saw fit. As they obeyed the laws of the one true God, they were a blessing to others. They were free to declare what the Spirit of the Lord was saying to them that they might fulfill their destiny to bless all the people of the earth because of the liberty they enjoyed. In such an environment of liberty, Jacob (Israel) spoke a blessing over his son Joseph. Jacob spoke the blessing of his grandfather Abraham over his son, as it was an everlasting blessing. Because of the blood of Jesus, this blessing was not just for the people of Israel, but for whosoever would receive it regardless of race, culture, gender, national origin, or anything else. Everyone qualifies as a "whosoever."

> *"And I will make of thee a great nation, and I will bless thee, and make thy name great; and thou shalt be a blessing: And I will bless them that bless thee, and curse him that curseth thee: and in thee shall all families of the earth be blessed."* (GENESIS 12:2-3)

> *"And if ye be Christ's, then are ye Abraham's seed, and heirs according to the promise." (GALATIANS 3:29)*

The Spirit of the Lord brings liberty. Liberty enables the people of God to walk in the blessings of Abraham to bless the whole world. Liberty brings blessings and a higher standard of living. Liberty is from God. Our founders knew this. They even went as far as to have the following etched on the Liberty Bell: *"Proclaim liberty throughout all the land unto all the inhabitants thereof."* Those words came out of Leviticus 25:10.

God wants liberty for all people, but not all people will accept it. Because God gave us a free will, he cannot guarantee equal outcome for all people. God wants liberty, but people are free to reject the ways and thoughts of God. These folks think that they are smarter than God is; their foolishness is what brings them down to a lower level.

> *"I call heaven and earth to record this day against you, that I have set before you life and death, blessing and cursing: therefore choose life, that both thou and thy seed may live."* (DEUTERONOMY 30:19)

Rebelling against God and thinking opposite from God not only brings you down; it brings others down too as they are persuaded to think like a low-living, small-thinking, natural man. This will not bless others, but, rather brings failure, lack, and even death.

> *"There is a way which seemeth right unto a man, but the end thereof are the ways of death"* (PROVERBS 14:12 AND 16:25)

Many people in the U. S. today, like Esau, the son of Isaac, are willing to throw away their godly heritage for a "mess of pottage." In other words, they are willing to destroy the great heritage and destiny, given to them by God, as a citizen of the United States of America, just so they can have an immediate, temporary solution, or handout. They don't realize that they are not only throwing away their heritage, but the heritage of all of the citizens of the U. S. They don't understand that our freedom was bought with the price of blood and has been maintained with the shed blood of those who put themselves in harm's way so we can be free.

They have believed the lies of those who proclaim that they know how to govern without regard to the laws of God. Those who reject God think they should, for the most part, think for the people, without people having the liberty to think for themselves. These ruling elite believe they know what others should eat, what others should say, and even what kind of energy others should consume. They want their abundance to come off the backs of those who oppose them and from those who have been deceived into thinking they can't make it without government assistance. Those who believe they must have government assistance will continue to support the ones who promise greater assistance out of fear of losing their sustenance. Anything based on fear is not of God. This kind of fear does not come from God. God's kingdom is based on faith, not fear.

> *"For God hath not given us the spirit of fear; but of power, and of love, and of a sound mind."* (2 TIMOTHY 1:7)

Those who want to collapse the United States economy and its system of capitalism are carnally minded. They deceivingly state high moral intentions but really just want power. They don't care if the nation is destroyed and people suffer hardships, as long as they get power over people. They are deceived and mistakenly think that the wealth production will continue as before. They should study history and find that every previous socialist nation has brought great poverty to its people, and the government treasuries eventually end up empty.

All the activity of planning the end of capitalism is demonic in its origin. All of the socialistic forms of thinking and living that destroy liberty (communism, Marxism, liberation theology, Fabian Society, etc.) are contrary to the Word of God. They are from the flesh and they are carnal. To think in such as fashion is to be carnally minded.

> *"For they that are after the flesh do mind the things of the*

flesh; but they that are after the Spirit the things of the Spirit. For to be carnally minded is death; but to be spiritually minded is life and peace. Because the carnal mind is enmity against God: for it is not subject to the law of God, neither indeed can be. So then they that are in the flesh cannot please God." (ROMANS 8:5-8)

Our heavenly Father does not want his children to look to the government to take care of them. We are his people and he is our sole source of supply.

"But my God shall supply all your need according to his riches in glory by Christ Jesus" (PHILIPPIANS 4:19)

"Therefore take no thought, saying, What shall we eat? or, What shall we drink? or, Wherewithal shall we be clothed? (For after all these things do the Gentiles seek :) for your heavenly Father knoweth that ye have need of all these things. But seek ye first the kingdom of God, and his righteousness; and all these things shall be added unto you." (MATTHEW 6:31-33)

CHAPTER FOUR

CLOWARD AND PIVEN:
SETTING THE STAGE FOR ALINSKY'S *RULES FOR RADICALS*

Richard Cloward and Frances Fox Piven, husband and wife, were professors together at the Columbia University School of Social Work in the 1960s. Their strategy was developed in a May 1966 article in the liberal magazine *The Nation* entitled "The Weight of the Poor: A Strategy to End Poverty." The two stated that many Americans who were eligible for welfare were not receiving benefits, and that a welfare enrollment drive would strain local budgets, precipitating a crisis at the state and local levels that would be a wake-up call for the federal government, particularly the Democrat Party.

The Cloward and Piven strategy was inspired by the writings of Saul Alinsky in his book *Reveille for Radicals*, the forerunner of his next book, *Rules for Radicals*. Their strategy advocated the creation of a crisis so government can gain more control. More specifically, they strove to force political change through orchestrated crisis. Cloward and Piven advocated that if you can't create a real crisis; then fabricate a make-believe crisis.

The purpose of the strategy was to hasten the fall of capitalism by overloading the government bureaucracy with a flood of impossible demands, thus pushing society into crisis and economic collapse. Their goal was to replace the welfare system with a national system of "a guaranteed annual income and thus an end to poverty."

Cloward and Piven's article was focused on forcing the Democrat Party, which in 1966 controlled the presidency and both houses of the United States Congress, to take federal action to help the poor. They stated that full enrollment of those eligible for welfare "would produce bureaucratic disruption in welfare agencies and fiscal disruption in local and state governments" that would "deepen existing divisions among elements in the big city Democrat coalitions. As a result, the national Democrat Party would be constrained to advance a federal solution to poverty that would override local welfare failures.[5]

Cloward and Piven wanted to hijack the Democrat party as shown from these words from their article in the magazine *The Nation.*

"Conservative Republicans are always ready to declaim the evils of public welfare, and they would probably be the first to raise a hue and cry. But deeper and politically more telling conflicts would take place within the Democratic coalition... Whites – both working class ethnic groups and many in the middle class – would be aroused against the ghetto poor, while liberal groups, which until recently have been comforted by the notion that the poor are few...would probably support the movement. Group conflict, spelling political crisis for the local party apparatus, would thus become acute as welfare rolls mounted and the strains on the local budgets became more severe."

From 1965 to 1974, primarily due to the efforts of Cloward and Piven and their followers, the total welfare recipients in the U. S. went from 4.3 million people to 10.8 million people. In 1975, there were nearly one million welfare recipients in New York City alone. As a result, New York City declared bankruptcy that year.[6]

Cloward and Piven were inspired by the Watts riots in Los Angeles in 1965. They published their article, which explained the best and most efficient way to bring about a Saul Alinsky type social change to America. They directed the activists that followed them to shout about a crisis, even if one did not exist. If there was any predicament at all, even if it was far from threatening, they were to exaggerate it so that it appeared as very ominous.

The Cloward and Piven strategy is still taunting us today. Some examples might sound like this: There is a health care crisis! We need national healthcare! How about this for a crisis: global warming is destroying the planet! We will all burn up in fifty years! Other examples of an exaggerated crisis might apply to the automobile industry and the banking industry.

There was no real crisis in healthcare. We had the finest healthcare in the world by leaps and bounds. The costs were too high, but that was due to too much government regulation and too much government constraints on competition. We have not all burned up. In fact, temperatures have gone slightly down, yet are within the normal small fluctuations that have always taken place since temperatures have been recorded. Since the warming didn't transpire as "science" indicated that it would, they now call it climate change so the "crisis" can remain alive.

There have been no results from any studies that use the scientific method that indicate any abnormal changing trends in temperatures. There have been models developed to forecast temperatures 100 years from now. These unscrupulous "scientists" who have forsaken the scientific method, have simply adjusted their assumptions until they get the results they want to see.

I challenge anyone to show me a real scientific study using the scientific method that indicates any significant danger ahead from climate change. Do I believe in climate change? Sure I do. The climate changes every couple of hours here in Texas, but it is not dangerous to the survival of man. These loony-tune "scientists" want us to believe their 100-year forecast, and thus cower in fear when those very same people consistently miss 100-hour forecasts by a wide margin on a regular basis. Often times, they can't get a 100-minute forecast right.

The Cloward and Piven strategy was derived from Saul Alinsky's radical thinking, which was derived from the Fabian Society, which was inspired by Satan. There was no healthcare crisis but we have to have national healthcare. There is no climate change crisis, but let's destroy the coal and oil and gas industries, thus destroying thousands of jobs and putting our national security and our power grid security in great danger.

Destroying the healthcare, coal, and the oil and gas industries is how you "fundamentally transform" a nation from strength to weakness. It is a demonic plan to thwart the U.S.A. from fulfilling its kingdom destiny. Five days before he was inaugurated in January 2009, Barack Obama said the following: "We are five days away from fundamentally transforming the United States of America."

Here is a quote from Cloward and Piven's article defining a crisis: "By crisis, we mean a publicly visible disruption in some institutional sphere."

Reacting to a crisis is the only way to bring about a new world order. All modern socialism has its roots in the Fabian Society notion that the elites control the lives of the common man. The Fabian Society further believes that the world or a nation must be destroyed so it can be rebuilt into the twisted vision of people like Shaw, Wells, Sanger, Cloward, Piven, Alinsky, Obama, Hillary Clinton, and the financier of all disrupting agents, the New World Order's current leading advocate, George Soros.

George Soros may very well be the most evil man currently residing on earth. It is amazing to hear him talk about his days as a teenager when he helped Nazi agents seize property of Jews because they wouldn't need it where they were going (the gas chambers). Here is what Soros said in reflecting on his time in seizing property from Jews.

"It was actually, probably, the happiest time of my life, that year of German occupation. For me, it was a very positive experience. It's a strange thing, because you see incredible suffering around you; it's a very happy making, exhilarating experience."

Soros said in his book *The Age of Flexibility,* referring to his quest to control the world, that "the main obstacle to a stable and just world order is the United States." It must be because we have that pesky Constitution. Soros has stated that what he has done in other countries to overthrow governments, he will do in this country.

Here is what Hillary Clinton says about George Soros.

"Our country needs help. We need people like George Soros, who is fearless, and willing to step up when it counts." To her, Alinsky is great and Soros is great and therefore the American people and their liberties must mean nothing to her.

The Cloward and Piven strategy helped set the stage for Saul Alinsky's next book, the playbook of the current, modern socialists, *Rules for Radicals.* This book set the stage for high hopes for a new world order for a George Soros open society without borders. That is why Soros sent paid agitators from Moveon.org to disrupt Donald Trump rallies because Trump wants to secure the border. Borders stop the new world order. The devil has always been against nations with borders.

Without a doubt, Cloward and Piven, influenced by Alinsky, kept the Fabian dream alive and set the stage for Alinsky's "masterpiece" *Rules for Radicals.* Alinsky's new book inspired the likes of Barack Obama and Hillary Clinton. It set the atmosphere for George Soros to be the puppet master (a term coined by Glenn Beck).

Soros funds the following organizations: Open Society Institute, the Tides Foundation, Center for American

Progress, Democracy Alliance Group, Moveon.org, Media Matters, and more. Millions of dollars run back and forth between the groups to fund progressive candidates, but much of the money eventually goes to Moveon.org to fund demonstrations or to Media Matters to give twisted and false stories to various media outlets to disseminate lies to foster the overthrow of the U.S.A.

Before we get to the Alinsky playbook in the next chapter, let's take a little time to talk about borders. To have an open society without borders, you need socialism. In God's plan, each person is unique and has a unique kingdom destiny to fulfill with the free will to say yes or no to God. We read earlier from Genesis chapter 11 where God rejected man's attempt to have no borders in a society where every one of the common folk would be the same.

If God had not dispersed them through the confusion of their language, most of the entire population would have ended up working for the Babylonian government, building the devil's system, and working for slave wages to fulfill the vision of a few ruling elite.

What did the Babylonian system want to do? Verse 4 of chapter 11 tells that they wanted to build a city, build a tower in that city that reached to heaven, make a name for themselves, and not to be scattered across the earth. Building a city was just a way not to be dispersed. Building a tower to reach heaven was just a way to make a name for themselves. Both of these goals were totally opposite of the will of God then, and are still in rebellion against God today.

Making a name is all about regarding the approval of men more than the approval of God. If they valued the approval of God, they would have dispersed to replenish the earth. They built a city so that they wouldn't have to disperse. They needed the security of man rather than trust the goodness and faithfulness of God. Dispersing meant leaving the security of man and trusting in God for their security. They would have to leave the common provision and seek their own kingdom destiny. Little did they know that the common provision is the lowest level of provision that there is. For after the ruling elite get their share, there is very little left to share in common. They didn't realize that God had a unique, wonderful plan to profit each one of them.

> *"And they sung a new song, saying, Thou art worthy to take the book, and to open the seals thereof: for thou wast slain, and hast redeemed us to God by thy blood out of every kindred, and tongue, and people, and nation;"* (REVELATION 5:9)

It's a beautiful thing to see the different nations with their various languages, music, architectures, cuisines, climates, landscapes, scenery and markets. All of these unique people and nations have been invited by Jesus to become joint heirs with him. God separated the nations so that people would have the best chance to enter into the kingdom of God. Each person is a unique "whosoever."

> *"For God so loved the world, that he gave his only begotten Son, that whosoever believeth in him should not perish, but have everlasting life. For God sent not his Son into the world to condemn the world; but that the world through him might be saved."* (JOHN 3:16-17)

God separated the people into various nations because he doesn't want a global currency or a global language and certainly not a global government. God went out of his way to prevent a new world order or an open society without borders.

> *"Go to, let us go down, and there confound their language, that they may not understand one another's speech. So the LORD scattered them abroad from thence upon the face of all the earth: and they left off to build the city."* (GENESIS 11:7-8)

> *"From one man he made all the nations, that they should inhabit the whole earth; and he marked out their appointed times in history and the boundaries of their lands. God did this so that they would seek him and perhaps reach out for him and find him, though he is not far from any one of us."* (ACTS 17:26-27 NIV)

> *"Do not move an ancient boundary stone set up by your ancestors."* (PROVERBS 22:28 NIV)

> *"You gave them kingdoms and nations, allotting to them even the remotest frontiers."* (NEHEMIAH 9:22A NIV)

Whenever there is a global society, the potential for a global crisis is greater. Today, people try to create a global crisis in order to achieve evil plans that entail manifesting power over people, convincing them that they are "bricks" and not "stones." They create an illusion that the normal challenges of life are too big and too complicated, and only the brilliant leaders of government have the answers.

Remember, you are as unique as a stone and you are made to glorify God in a special way. No one else can do what you do. You are not a brick. In Jesus, you are a precious, beautiful, living stone.

> *"Coming to Him as to a living stone, rejected indeed by men, but chosen by God and precious, you also, as living stones, are being built up a spiritual house, a holy priesthood, to offer up spiritual sacrifices acceptable to God through Jesus Christ."* (1 Peter 2:4-5 NKJV)

CHAPTER FIVE

SAUL ALINSKY AND *RULES FOR RADICALS*

The first thing to know and remember about *Rules for Radicals* is that it is dedicated to Lucifer. Alinsky thought that Lucifer was really neat the way he rebelled against God and that he should be emulated. The book offers tips on how to organize for a change to socialism by using various types of tactics. According to Alinsky, the end justifies the means. Lying, deceit and corruption are acceptable. As to lying, the strategy is to keep saying the same lie over and over until it is accepted as the truth.

According to Alinsky's rules, you attack individuals, not ideas. That is a key element. You identify a target and go after it. Another tactic is the use of language. You change the way you identify certain things to make them more palatable to the general public. Spending has now become referred to as "investing," taxes are now called "contributions," and abortion is a "choice." According to Alinsky, people must be unhappy, frustrated, and without hope so they will throw away their freedoms for a "mess of pottage" in the present. Below are some quotes from *Rules for Radicals*:

> "Socialism wants to ingrain certain beliefs into society and those thoughts can best be fostered by community organizations."

> "An organizer must stir up dissatisfaction and discontent: provide a channel into which the people can angrily pour out their frustrations. You pit the haves against the have-nots."

> "The first step in community organization is community disorganization."

> "An organizer working in and for an open society is in an ideological dilemma to begin with, he does not have a fixed truth. Truth to him is relative and changing: everything to him is relative."

According to the Bible, the truth never changes.

> "Jesus said to him, "I am the way, the truth, and the life. No one comes to the Father except through Me." (JOHN 14:6 NKJV)

> "Jesus Christ the same yesterday, and today, and forever." (HEBREWS 13:8)

> "Forever, O LORD, thy word is settled in heaven" (PSALM 119:89)

> "The grass withereth, the flower fadeth: but the word of our God shall stand forever." (ISAIAH 40:8)

"Heaven and earth shall pass away, but my words shall not pass away." (MATTHEW 24:35 NIV)

Satan and the socialists don't want you to know the truth because they don't want you free to obey God. To limit your freedom, they must limit your knowledge of the truth. That's why they teach there is no truth.

"And ye shall know the truth, and the truth shall make you free." (JOHN 8:32)

It is inconceivable to me to think that a Christian would want to follow a man or a woman who praises and follows a man who praises and follows Lucifer. That is exactly what people are doing when they vote for and support Barack Obama or Hillary Clinton. Alinsky's role model is Lucifer. Barack Obama and Hillary Clinton's role model is Alinsky.

Alinsky, in his book, *Rules for Radicals*, explains his purpose for writing his book: "What follows is for those who want to change the world from what is to what they believe it should be. *The Prince* was written by Machiavelli for the Haves on how to hold power. *Rules for Radicals* is written for the Have-Nots on how to take it away."

This hearkens back to the Fabian Society premise that you must destroy others and society in order to rebuild or remold it nearer to your heart's desire or what you believe it should be. There is no belief in a loving God from whom all blessings flow and there is no belief that there is no shortage in the Kingdom of God and that there is plenty to go around. It's that same old lie from the devil that the world is a zero-sum game and that for somebody to gain, someone else must lose. For someone else to have, someone else has to be a have-not.

You can see where Obama's Marxist attitude comes from. This book is where the notion of "hope and change" came from.

"The organizer's job is to inseminate an invitation for himself, to agitate, introduce ideas, get people pregnant with hope and a desire for change and to identify you as the person most qualified for this purpose." - Saul Alinsky, *Rules for Radicals*

Rules for Radicals has thirteen rules for power tactics. There are eleven rules for ethics and means. We need to at least take a peek at the thirteen power tactics, because we are not to be ignorant of the devil's devices. Here is a part of Alinsky's introduction to his tactics:

"Here our concern is with the tactic of taking; how the Have-Nots can take power away from the Haves. For an elementary illustration of tactics, take parts of your face as the point of reference; your eyes, your ears, and your nose. First the eyes; if you have organized a vast, mass-based people's organization, you can parade it visibly before the enemy and openly show your power. Second the ears; if your organization is small in numbers, then ... conceal the members in the dark but raise a din and clamor that will make the listener believe that your organization numbers many more than it does. Third, the nose; if your organization is too tiny even for noise, stink up the place."

Let's take a quick look at the thirteen rules for power tactics.

1. "Power is not only what you have, but what the enemy thinks you have." Alinsky explains that power and authority comes from two main sources, namely, people and money. The Bible declares that all power and authority comes from God.

> *"And Jesus came and spoke unto them, saying, "All power is given unto Me in Heaven and on earth."* (MATTHEW 28:18)
>
> *"And when he had called unto him his twelve disciples, he gave them power against unclean spirits, to cast them out, and to heal all manner of sickness and all manner of disease." (MATTHEW 10:1)*

2. "Never go outside the expertise of your people. When an action or tactic is outside the experience of the people, the result is confusion, fear, and retreat. It also means a collapse of communication."

3. "Wherever possible go outside of the experience of the enemy. Here you want to cause confusion, fear, and retreat."

4. "Make the enemy live up to their own book of rules. You can kill them with this, for they can no more obey their own rules than the Christian church can live up to Christianity". Alinsky further clarifies this rule with the following words:

"When pressed to honor every word of every law and statute, every Judeo-Christian moral tenet, and every implicit promise of the liberal social contract, human agencies inevitably fall short. The system's failure to "live up" to its rule book can then be used to discredit it altogether, and to replace the capitalist "rule book" with a socialist one."

This clearly demonstrates the connection with Cloward and Piven to overwhelm the system, which connects to the Fabians to destroy the system and remold it into a socialistic one with a small class of ruling elites, thus eliminating the middle class that they pretend to love so much.

Rule 5. "Ridicule is man's most potent weapon. It is almost impossible to counterattack ridicule. Also it infuriates the opposition, who then react to your advantage."

Rule 6. "A good tactic is one that your people enjoy. If your people are not having a ball doing it, there is something very wrong with the tactic."

Rule 7. "A tactic that drags on too long becomes a drag. Man can sustain militant interest in any issue for only a limited time, after which it becomes a ritualistic commitment, like going to church on Sunday mornings. New issues and crises are always developing, and one's reaction becomes, 'Well, my heart bleeds for those people and I'm all for the boycott, but after all there are other important things in life'—and there it goes."

Rule 8. "Keep the pressure on, with different tactics and actions, and utilize all events of the period for your purpose." Alinsky encourages his radically minded group of followers to keep trying new things to keep the opposition off balance. They are to attack from all sides and never give the opposition a chance to rest, regroup, recover and re-strategize.

Rule 9. "The threat is usually more terrifying than the thing itself." Alinsky believed that the imagination can dream up many more consequences than any activist.

Rule 10. "The major premise for tactics is the development of operations that will maintain a constant pressure upon the opposition. It is this unceasing pressure that results in the reactions from the opposition that are essential for the success of the campaign. It should be remembered not only that the action is in the reaction but that action is itself the consequence of reaction and of reaction to the reaction, ad infinitum. The pressure produces the reaction, and constant pressure sustains action."

Rule 11. "If you push a negative hard and deep enough it will break through into its counterside; this is based on the principle that every positive has its negative."

Rule 12. "The price of a successful attack is a constructive alternative. You cannot risk being trapped by the enemy in his sudden agreement with your demand and saying 'You're right—we don't know what to do about this issue. Now you tell us.'

Rule 13. "Pick the target, freeze it, personalize it, and polarize it." Alinsky teaches his followers to go after people and not institutions because people can be hurt faster than institutions.

The main thrust of Alinsky's rules for ethics is simply this: anything goes. There is no morality. The end always justifies the means as we discussed earlier in the introduction. Alinsky believed that the best barometer of the effectiveness of a tactic is in direct proportion to how much the means is criticized as unethical. Here are some more quotes from *Rules for Radicals*.

"Don't worry if they call you names. The job of an organizer is to maneuver and bait the establishment so that it will publicly attack him as a dangerous enemy."

"An organizer dedicated to changing the life of a particular community must first rub raw the resentments of the people of the community; fan the latent hostilities of many of the people to the point of overt expression."

"The enemy properly goaded and guided in his reaction will be your major strength."

Alinsky did an interesting interview with *Playboy Magazine* where he revealed how he learned many of his tactics from mafia bosses like Frank Nitti, who was Al Capone's right hand man. Alinsky said he was fascinated with the mafia's ability to keep an iron fist on power in the community. Here is a short excerpt from the interview which was done shortly before Alinsky's death.

Playboy: "Do you believe in any kind of afterlife?"

Alinsky: "Let's say that if there is an afterlife, and I have anything to say about it, I will unreservedly choose to go to hell."

Playboy: "Why?"

Alinsky: "Hell would be heaven for me. All my life I've been with the have-nots. Over here, if you're a have-not, you're short of dough. If you're a have-not in hell, you're short of virtue. Once I get into hell, I'll start organizing the have-nots over there."

Playboy: "Why them?"

Alinsky: "They're my kind of people."

His comments are so sad. They show those of us who have been saved by grace through faith in Jesus Christ that we need to be more aggressive in letting everyone know that salvation is free for everyone, even those who are "short" on virtue.

> *"For God so loved the world, that he gave his only begotten Son, that whosoever believeth in him should not perish, but have everlasting life. For God sent not his Son into the world to condemn the world; but that the world through him might be saved."* (JOHN 3:16-17)

Hell is not like how the devil conveys it to his followers. There will be no wild parties and there will be no community to organize. It will consist of perpetual, eternal torment.

> *"where their worm dieth not, and the fire is not quenched."* (MARK 9:44)

CHAPTER SIX
CLOWARD AND PIVEN'S DREAM COMES TRUE

Cloward and Piven dreamed of the mindset of the collective taking control of the Democrat party. They dreamed of a party where faith in God was eliminated and every effort and deed was for the collective good and individual destinies regarded with disdain. Their dream was fully realized when Barack Obama, an advocate of liberation theology (a form of collectivism), became the Democrat party nominee and eventually the president of the United States.

Liberation theology extols the virtues of forced wealth redistribution and injects theology into the concept of "social justice." Liberation theology will leave people without Christ and destined to be in torment for all eternity, as its basic tenet is collective salvation and not individual salvation. In this philosophy, to obtain collective salvation, people must redistribute wealth "fairly" among the collective group. This is the "salvation" Barack Obama received through his pastor of twenty years, Jeremiah Wright. On several occasions, President Obama has stated that his individual salvation is based on the collective salvation of everyone.

President Obama also stated that individual salvation is based on collective salvation in his August 9, 1995, interview with Bill Thompson about his book *Dreams From My Father*. He made the same statement at the Campus Progress Conference on July 12, 2006, at Northwestern University on October 24, 2006, at Southern New Hampshire University on May 19, 2007, at Wesleyan University on May 25, 2008, and on many other occasions including those at Knox College, Xavier University, and the University of Chicago School of Medicine.[7] Liberation theology calls for political liberation rather than spiritual salvation. This theology is erroneous, as each one of us must stand alone before God.

> *"I the LORD search the heart, I try the reins, even to give every man according to his ways, and according to the fruit of his doings."* (JEREMIAH 17:10)

> *"For we must all appear before the judgment seat of Christ; that every one may receive the things done in his body, according to that he hath done, whether it be good or bad."* (2 CORINTHIANS 5:10)

> *"For the Son of man shall come in the glory of his Father with his angels; and then he shall reward every man according to his works."* (MATHEW 16:27)

> *"And before him shall be gathered all nations: and he shall separate them one from another, as a shepherd divideth his sheep from the goats: And he shall set the sheep on his right hand, but the goats on the left."* (MATHEW 25:32)

What the collectivists (socialists, Marxists, etc.) declare is best for the collective never turns out good for anyone except the small group of ruling elites who want to plan and run the lives of the rest of us. They try to blame all problems on the one percent who aren't "sharing" fairly with the common folk. The truth is that they don't care about the common man; they merely want to transfer the wealth into their hands (because they promise they will distribute it fairly). In doing so, they will replace the current one percent to be the new one percent who will control every aspect of our lives.

You see, the workings of our government are important to God because government is not just a political or cultural phenomenon; it is an important spiritual force for good or evil. In fact, the cosmic battle between God and Satan is a clash between two kingdoms or governments. When Jesus walked the earth in a body, he only preached about or taught about the kingdom of God, otherwise known as the kingdom of heaven. He did not come to establish a religion, but his kingdom or government.

> *"And Jesus went about all Galilee, teaching in their synagogues, and preaching the gospel of the kingdom, and healing all manner of sickness and all manner of disease among the people.* (MATTHEW 4:23*)*
>
> *"But if I cast out devils by the Spirit of God, then the kingdom of God is come unto you." (MATTHEW 12:28)*
>
> *"But seek first his kingdom and his righteousness, and all these things will be given to you as well." (MATTHEW 6:33 NIV)*

According to Jesus, the highest priority was seeking, knowing and living by his government, the kingdom of God. That's how you get all those other things by serving and giving to others. Isn't that wonderful? One of the best things about it is that there is no sorrow attached to those "things." You may acquire "things" by the way of the kingdom of darkness, but there is sorrow attached to them. Not so for the kingdom of God.

> *"The blessing of the LORD, it maketh rich, and he addeth no sorrow with it."* (PROVERBS 10:22)

Jesus spent all of his last forty days teaching the apostles exclusively about the kingdom of God. That message must have been of the utmost importance if it consumed the final forty days of his ministry on earth. It was the last thing they were to hear from Jesus.

> *"Until the day in which he was taken up, after that he through the Holy Ghost had given commandments unto the apostles whom he had chosen: To whom also he shewed himself alive after his passion by many infallible proofs, being seen of them forty days, and speaking of the things pertaining to the kingdom of God:"* (Acts 1:2-3)

It is clear from Scripture that there are two kingdoms operating in the world that we live in. There is the kingdom of darkness, also known as the world system or the Babylonian system. This kingdom or system of government wars against the system of the kingdom of light, also known as the kingdom of God or the kingdom of heaven.

> *"The Father, who has qualified you to share in the inheritance of his holy people in the kingdom of light. For he has rescued us from the dominion of darkness and brought us into the kingdom of the Son he loves."* (COLOSSIANS 1:12-13)

> *"For unto us a child is born, unto us a son is given: and the government shall be upon his shoulder: and his name shall be called Wonderful, Counseller, The mighty God, The everlasting Father, The Prince of Peace."* (ISAIAH 9:6)

When we enter the kingdom of God, we become part of the government of God as ambassadors for Jesus our king. As part of the government of God, and having been delivered from the dominion of the kingdom of darkness, we are to take dominion over the world system and make it on earth as it is in heaven. We should not accept the lie that there is nothing we can do to stop what is happening to our nation.

In other words, it is time to stop taking wooden nickels from the devil. That means not only stop being passive against the world system but stop helping the devil by declaring it must be the judgment of God on our nation. I have heard many preachers say that if God doesn't judge America then he will have to apologize to Sodom and Gomorrah. Excuse me, but God said that he would spare those cities if he could find ten righteous men.

> *"And Abraham drew near, and said, Wilt thou also destroy the righteous with the wicked?... And he said, Oh let not the Lord be angry, and I will speak yet but this once: Peradventure ten shall be found there. And he said, I will not destroy it for ten's sake."* (GENESIS 18:23,32)

Are there not more than ten righteous men in the United States of America? There are tens of millions of men who have been made righteous by the blood of Jesus. You see, 2 Chronicles 7:14 does not pertain to the non-covenant people but only to God's people. We can't rely on the actions of the ungodly to turn our nation around. It is up to those of us who are born again who are called by Christ's name.

I have witnessed a great outpouring of God's spirit. I have heard about, witnessed, and participated in a great many prayer gatherings all over America interceding for our nation. God's people have continuously stood in the gap for our nation and repented for our nation and called on the name of Jesus to heal our land anyway he wants to. God is faithful. He said that if we did that he would hear and heal our land. So stop fighting against God on the devil's team. If you are doing that, you need to repent and change your words and ways, especially if you are a preacher.

"If my people, which are called by my name, shall humble themselves, and pray, and seek my face, and turn from their wicked ways; then will I hear from heaven, and will forgive their sin, and will heal their land." (2 CHRONICLES 7:14)

Jesus told us to preach good news. Preachers, stop criticizing people for preaching only good news and not the bad news. Jesus didn't say preach good news and bad news. He said preach good news for the Bible is a book of good news. If you don't know that then you need more revelation about the information it contains.

The good news of the kingdom is the good news that Jesus preached about. Jesus did not preach bad news. He preached the gospel (good news) of the kingdom of God. Its evil counterpart, the kingdom of darkness (the world system) wants to remove God from our lives and guide a bunch of "useful idiots" to strive to reach Utopia on our own merits with strategies just like what was found in *Rules for Radicals.*

We cannot fall prey to this evil plan. We desperately need leadership in this nation that does not follow a book dedicated to Satan as Hillary Clinton and Barack Obama do. Instead, we need leaders who follow a Constitution dedicated to Jesus Christ. Godly leaders value the people they lead. The people are not useful idiots to them, but precious people who they want to see prosperous and safe from harm.

They follow the example of Jesus to love those that follow them. They don't withhold from them and exclude them; they include them. Think about what Jesus did. He allowed us to be joint heirs with him. Jesus knew that there is plenty to go around and that the notion of a zero-sum game is nonsense. When great challenges come, leaders who follow the example of Jesus and value the people will uplift their people with words and actions.

Think about how Winston Churchill led the people of Great Britain during the German's bombing of London in World War Two. He challenged the British people and told them that they would never surrender. When France fell and England was next on Hitler's list and the bombs began to fall, Churchill said the following to rally the people of Britain: "Let us therefore brace ourselves to our duties, and so bear ourselves that if the British Empire and its Commonwealth last for a thousand years, men will still say, 'This was their finest hour.'"

Compare that to what President Obama said after the

ISIS shootings in Paris. He said, "It's a setback." After Major Nidal Hassan shot up Fort Hood while shouting *Allahu Akbar*, what did Obama call it? "Workplace violence." After the shootings in Orlando, the president still could not bring himself to say the words "radical Islamic terrorism.' He merely called it a hate crime. He tried to deny any connection between the attack and Islam. He only saw the incident as a "crisis" that brought an opportunity to hawk gun control.

President Obama won't even recognize that ISIS is an Islamic terrorist organization, even though the "I" in ISIS stands for Islamic. Why does everyone in the Obama administration call it ISIL? Let's talk about what the initials in ISIS and ISIL stand for. ISIS stands for Islamic State in Iraq and Syria. ISIL stands for Islamic State in Iraq and the Levant.

The Levant is an area that covers Cypress, Israel, Jordan, Lebanon, Palestine and Syria. It also covers parts of Egypt and Turkey. No matter what expert you ask, they will all say that the Levant covers all of the territory God gave to Abraham that is listed in the Book of Genesis. Islamic leaders who hate Israel want a caliphate that includes all the land that God said was for the descendants of Abraham, Isaac, and Jacob. Islamists say it is for the descendants of Ishmael, just like they erroneous believe that Abraham, by faith, offered up Ishmael, not Isaac.

When Obama uses the term ISIL, it is code to the Muslim world that he is one of them, or at least that he places higher regard for the Muslim sharia law than he does for the United States and its Constitution. Obama said his goal was to degrade and destroy ISIS, yet we see absolutely no evidence of any efforts to do so. That is because his goal is not to degrade and destroy ISIS, but, rather, to degrade and destroy the United States of America. It has to be destroyed so it can be remolded closer to his heart's desire.

He is so ashamed of our glorious history that he has to offer apologies for it to terrorists. In an effort to justify murders by ISIS terrorists, he actually said that they had "legitimate grievances" against our country. What possible grievances could they have that could justify mass murders? It must be that terrible western way of life that offends them. I'll tell you what offends me, Mr. President—the senseless evil slaughter of innocent American lives.

The president's higher regard for sharia law over our Constitution was demonstrated when he humiliated our nation when he bowed to the Saudi King. This unspeakable act can be seen on you tube if you search "Obama bows." Concerning the shootings in Orlando, Obama does not find fault with the aspect of sharia law that says homosexuals must die. Rather, he finds fault with the laws from our Constitution giving us the right to bear arms.

Yes, Cloward and Piven's dream for the Democrat party has come true. The Democrat party has become a vessel for the kingdom of darkness as it has been hijacked by radicals. In an attempt to win elections for perpetuity, they have welcomed radical factions from socialists, communists, LGBT activists, proponents of total amnesty for illegal aliens, open border advocates, only black lives matter crowd, murderers of babies, Agenda 21 proponents, collectivists, haters of Israel, Islamic terrorists, and all those who hate God, the Constitution, freedom, our heritage, and our way of life.

The Republicans are almost as bad. While the Democrats have openly included all the wrong people, the Republicans have tried to secretly reject all the right people. It started out as subtle, but now I think the cat is out of the bag. It has become obvious to me, at least, that the Republican establishment really doesn't like Tea Party types and Libertarians. These are the people that should be included in leadership, not rejection. The GOP establishment sees these patriotic Americans as a nuisance instead of the answer to their problems. At least the Republicans don't want to kick God out of their platform, and they still welcome words that honor God.

If you still have any doubts that Democrats want to remove God from government and from our lives, I turn your attention to the Democrat National Convention of 2012. A motion was put forth to include the words that God is central to the American story and Jerusalem is the capital of Israel. This was done to quiet criticism they were receiving from the previous day when they eliminated all mention of God from their platform. The attempt to add these words into their 2012 platform required a 2/3 majority vote. The first vote revealed more no votes than aye votes. The chairman presiding over the vote seemed visibly shaken and asked for another vote.

The second audible vote revealed an even greater margin of no votes to aye votes. The chairman began to sweat and was so distraught that he asked for one last vote. Again, the no votes overwhelmed the aye votes. The chairman, determined to pass the motion, declared that the motion had passed. Immediately, the majority of delegates cried loud boos that rang out over those assembled inside the Time Warner Cable Arena. Search "Democrats Boo God" on YouTube and watch it for yourself.

In essence, the Democrat party openly mocked God. It gives me hope that God will intervene to stop what the devil is doing through the Democrats, because I know the Scriptures.

> *"Be not deceived; God is not mocked: for whatsoever a man soweth, that shall he also reap."* (GALATIANS 6:7)

How do we withstand this onslaught from the devil using the Democrat party to strip us of our freedoms to live for God? We must resist the devil while still loving our enemies, stagger not at the promises of God, and speak those promises as we call things that are not as though they were. If we do these things, the victory shall be ours.

> *"Now thanks be unto God, which always causeth us to triumph in Christ, and maketh manifest the savour of his knowledge by us in every place."* (2 CORINTHIANS 2:14)

CHAPTER SEVEN

AGENDA 21 AND PHONY ENVIRONMENTALISM

"And God blessed them, and God said unto them, Be fruitful, and multiply, and replenish the earth, and subdue it: and have dominion over the fish of the sea, and over the fowl of the air, and over every living thing that moveth upon the earth. And God said, Behold, I have given you every herb bearing seed, which is upon the face of all the earth, and every tree, in the which is the fruit of a tree yielding seed; to you it shall be for meat. And to every beast of the earth, and to every fowl of the air, and to every thing that creepeth upon the earth, wherein there is life, I have given every green herb for meat: and it was so. And God saw every thing that he had made, and, behold, it was very good. And the evening and the morning were the sixth day." (GENESIS 1:28-31)

God said subdue the earth and have dominion over it and all the animals and all the plants, as they were given for man's food and man's use, and God said that was very good. Many environmentalists today declare that animals and plants are more important than man and that we should submit to them as their lives are a higher priority than the lives of men, women, boys, and girls.

Many have the point of view that it is appropriate to slaughter an innocent child, but there is hell to pay for shooting Cecil the lion. That kind of thinking is demonic in origin as the devil is angry that the blood of Jesus put the dominion of the earth back in the hands of God's people after it was forfeited to the devil by Adam through disobedience.

These phony environmentalists don't care about the environment; they just want to follow the devil's plan to make life hard for man. Remember the Luciferian goal to destroy the world in order to remold it with elites planning the lives of the rest of us. It's not about protecting the environment; it is about gaining control over you. They are like their father the devil who masquerades as an angel of light and as a wolf in sheep's clothing. They want us to think that what they are doing is out of love and for our own good.

> *"For such are false apostles, deceitful workers, transforming themselves into the apostles of Christ. And no marvel; for Satan himself is transformed into an angel of light. Therefore it is no great thing if his ministers also be transformed as the ministers of righteousness; whose end shall be according to their works."* (2 CORINTHIANS 11:13-15)

Phony environmentalism is one of the major ways used by the devil for the purpose of ushering in the premise that we all must give up our individuality and unite to serve the "greater good" in order to save mother earth. This is the strategy used by United Nations Agenda 21. The end game is for us to eliminate the God of Abraham from our lives in this new world order.

"No one will enter the New World Order unless he or she will make a pledge to worship Lucifer. No one will enter the New Age unless he will take a Luciferian Initiation."- David Spangler, Director of Planetary Initiative, United Nations Agenda 21

You won't have the right to freely worship as you, individually, see fit. You will have no individual rights because it is all about the collective. "Individual rights will have to take a back seat to the collective." - Harvey Ruvin, Vice Chair of the International Council on Local Environmental Initiatives (ICLEI)

Let's talk about ICLEI (pronounced ick-lee). It is a non-governmental spin-off of the United Nations to implement Agenda 21 locally across the world. It is a membership organization for cities; 7,807 worldwide as of 2012. Headquartered in Bonn, Germany, it is a lobbying and policy group that is intended to influence and change local governmental policies related to all aspects of human life. It designs and sells systems that monitor, report, and control water and energy usage. This information is then shared.

By concentrating power in cities, this group circumvents requirements for ratification of international treaties and gives the illusion of local control. ICLEI is structured as a parallel government but has no transparency because it is a private non-profit. In fact, the cities then ally in regional conglomerates which break jurisdictional boundaries and will destroy local control. These regional boards are unelected and not answerable to the citizenry. Ultimately, this facilitates global governance by invalidating individual cities, counties, states, and nations with agreements and interwoven systems to which they are bound by contract via public private partnerships.[8]

The one-world-government folks who foster no individual rights are coming at us from the top down (U.N. Agenda 21) and the bottom up (ICLEI). As people in America began to find out about ICLEI, they became furious and began to inquire of their city governments if they were members of ICLEI. The organization promptly changed its name to Local Governments for Sustainability and deleted its page on its website that contained the listing of its member cities in the U.S.A. This took place in 2012.

Agenda 21 is all about the term "sustainable development." Agenda 21 is the 1992 United Nations declaration on the environment and development. This was done in a U.N. meeting in Rio de Janeiro, Brazil. Our President George H.W. Bush was there participating in this foolishness. Even before Agenda 21 was established, he had spoken many times about a new world order. This is not strictly a Democrat problem. In fact, there is a very good organization called Democrats Against U.N. Agenda 21.

Agenda 21 is supposedly the agenda for the twenty-first century with a brave new world, or a new world order without borders, where most everything that Christians and other decent people cherish and hold dear will no longer exist. I'm talking about such things as worshipping God, individual liberties, and the US Constitution.

Agenda 21 elevates nature above man. It contains something called the precautionary principle that states that you are guilty until proven innocent. That is how they will keep freedom-loving people in check. Sustainable development is the philosophy designed to bring people across the world under the full control of a small, elite group. Agenda 21 is a forty-chapter document about how to control the world and thereby putting the world once again in the hands of Satan.

It is based entirely upon socialist control and ideals. Sustainable developers have designed a global movement to create a world government in accordance with certain objectives. These objectives include: the abolition of private property, an end to national sovereignty, the abandonment of inalienable, God-given rights described in the Constitution, the restructure of the family unit, limits on individual opportunity, and restrictions on mobility and transportation.[9]

The goal of sustainable development is to eliminate the middle class. There are the elites and then the commoners. There is no individuality among the commoners. They are not considered lively stones, but bricks, as all commoners are just like the others. The following items are deemed to be unsustainable in Agenda 21's green goals and thus must be eliminated for commoners: private property, fossil fuels, consumerism, irrigation, golf courses, ski lodges, paved roads, commercial agriculture, farm lands, pastures, grazing of livestock, air conditioning, and last but not least, the family unit.[10]

This is not a joke to be laughed off. The written goal clearly states that human beings are to be concentrated into human settlement zones. Education is to be centered on the environment as the central organizing principle. Later, in chapter eight, we will focus more on the demonic goals of education called Common Core that is part of this evil agenda.

Support for these crazy ideas has come from George H. W. Bush, Bill Clinton, Barack Obama and Hillary Clinton. Let's start with Bush and we will get to the others later. The senior Bush made the following comments in 1992 while addressing the U.N. during the conference in Rio de Janeiro:

> *"It is the sacred principles enshrined in the United Nations Charter to which the American people will henceforth pledge their allegiance." - President George H. W. Bush*

When I saw this I couldn't believe my eyes. The United Nations demonic charter is sacred? What about our Constitution? This was said by a Republican! Boy, did he pull the wool over our eyes. In this 1992 U.N. conference, George H. W. Bush executed the Agenda 21 protocols on behalf of the United States and brought it back to Washington D.C. Within a year, President Clinton, by executive order with no congressional review, established the President's Council for Sustainable Development.

Let's compare the U.N. Declaration of Human Rights against the U.S. Declaration of Independence. According to the U.N. Declaration, the purpose of government is to control the individual for the greater good of a global community. It is stated this way, "Rights and freedoms may in no case be exercised contrary to the purposes and principles of the United Nations."

According to the U.S. Declaration, the purpose of government is to protect the inalienable rights of each individual. It is stated this way, "That all men are created equal, that they are endowed by their creator with certain inalienable rights."

The U.N. Declaration of Human Rights can be summarized as follows: Government grants, restricts or withdraws your rights according to your needs. You and the product of your labor belong to the community. The U.S. Declaration of Independence can be summarized as follows. You are born with rights. Government exists to protect them. You and the product of your labor belong to you.[11]

If you live in the suburbs today, you will not be able to live there under sustainable development of Agenda 21. Please search the internet for a map of Agenda 21's The Wildlands Project for the U.S.A. Most areas (probably where your house is now) will be off limits to human beings. These zones are strictly for the benefit of animals and mother earth. There is no resource development allowed and no human activity allowed. If you live there now, you would be forced to leave your house and all your belongings to have them just rot away.

Surrounding those areas will be areas that are highly regulated with limited human activity. If you live there now, you must abandon your house and all your property. These two zones make up virtually all the area of the United States. There are just a few dots on the map representing smart growth zones. Humans (relegated lower than animals) will be stacked up in fourteen story buildings with stacks of small living unit boxes along railroad tracks. The smart growth program has jobs assigned with children cared for by the state.

If the global, sustainable developers reach their goals, the effect on the average American will be devastating. The ordinary American will live without independence, privacy, or any significant rights. Now you know why it is so important to Obama, Hillary Clinton, and other sustainable developers to implement gun controls. That's why a terrorist killing for Islam is not about Islam but about gun control. Never let a good crisis go to waste.

They must take your guns to be successful. There are too many rednecks here in Texas who own and know how to handle all kinds of guns. Sustainable developers will have to kill these citizens, for they will never leave their land. Agenda 21 believers will never get enough people to run them off their land. Casualties will be high and it would be the end of sustainable development. America, thank God for Texas, for if Agenda 21 gathers momentum it will be Texas that stops them if we can keep our guns. Therefore, cling to the second amendment no matter what. This agenda will never be fully implemented. In the spirit realm, we have the promises of God. In the natural, we have the Constitution, and if that is relegated to irrelevance, we have Texas rednecks with guns! Hallelujah!

Agenda 21 is defined by the United Nations as follows.

> *"A comprehensive plan of action to be taken globally, nationally, and locally by organizations of the United Nations' systems, governments and major groups in every area in which humans impact the environment."*

What a bunch of non sequitur baloney. Let me explain what Agenda 21 is really all about. The purpose of Agenda 21 and sustainable development is to have a small group of elites carry out centralized planning and control over every aspect of human life on planet Earth.

In 1992, Agenda 21 was officially adopted by approximately 178 nations, including the United States. It is a very ominous document. Starting in section one, it discusses wealth redistribution, changing consumption patterns, promoting health, population change, and sustainable settlement.

Here is a quote from the document as it relates to wealth redistribution:

"Developed countries and funding agencies should provide specific assistance to developing countries in adopting an enabling approach to the provision of shelter for all."

In other words, you don't need all that wealth. You won't have anything to spend it on anyway. That's right. We have to change our consumption patterns. There will be no car to drive, no malls to shop at, no ball games to go to, no movies to watch, and the list goes on. There will be no more air conditioning, as that is unsustainable. Very few showers will be allowed as showers use too much water, and by the way, there will be no hot showers as hot water takes energy. That is not sustainable. No sugary soft drinks, no matter how many ounces, because big brother knows best, so no more sugar for you.

That relates to the promoting of health because if you're

not healthy and productive the elites can't waste any of "their" resources on you. Population reduction will help make the human race sustainable as fewer people need fewer resources. Less people eliminate problems. It reminds me of what Joseph Stalin said, "No man, no problem."

Population will be reduced through sterilization, abortions, euthanasia and the destruction of the physically and mentally challenged. The population will be cleansed. The Agenda 21 depopulation goal is to bring the world's population from seven billion down to one billion by 2030. This is found in Agenda 21's United Nations Global Biodiversity Assessment Report on page 673 where it calls for the world's population to be reduced by 85%. That's a lot of exterminating of us undesirables who want freedom. That can't be accomplished by birth control. Here is a quote from the Initiative for the United Nations Eco 92 Earth Charter (Agenda 21 meeting):

> *"The present vast over population, now far beyond the world carrying capacity cannot be answered by future reductions in the birth rate due to contraception, sterilization and abortion, but must be met in the present by the reduction in the numbers presently existing. This must be done by whatever means necessary."*

Perhaps they will call on scientists to come up with a more humane gas to kill us and they will be polite as they do it. Aren't they wonderful? No, they are murdering butchers showing out as humanitarians. These people are sick. We have a presidential candidate, Hillary Clinton, who thinks that Agenda 21 and sustainability are great and congratulates Gro Harlem Brundtland for her great work in this area. Sound the alarm!

Who is behind Agenda 21? Where did it come from? Gro Harlem Brundtland, former Prime Minister of Norway and former Vice-President of Socialists International, was the originator of the term sustainable development. Gro is a very close friend of the Clintons and is very active in the Clinton Global Initiative, which has been shown to be very much fraudulent.

Hillary Clinton offered the following remarks to Gro Harlem Brundtland at a celebration for Gro on her seventieth birthday:

"As a former environment minister, a long-time advocate for sustainable development, and most recently as a United Nations special envoy for climate change, you helped set the stage for intensive diplomatic and scientific work being done on this issue today."

In 1987, Ms. Brundtland chaired the Brundtland Commission, which presented a report on sustainable development entitled *Our Common Future*. It was in this report that Gro coined the phrase "sustainable development," and the report provided the momentum for and was the forerunner of the U.N. Agenda 21 document. One of the forces behind Agenda 21 is our old friend, the Fabian Society, with its modern-day members and other like-minded groups and individuals up to their old tricks. There is nothing new under the sun.

Where does ICLEI (now Local Governments for Sustainability) and Agenda 21 get there funding and support? Mostly, the funding comes from George Soros. Through

The Open Society, Soros supports ICLEI and other Agenda 21 organizations. He also supports Agenda 21 organizations through the Apollo Alliance, which is part of the Tides Foundation, another Soros-funded organization.

The Apollo Alliance is the organization who prepared and gave us the Stimulus Bill to waste tax payer money for the purpose of funding progressive organizations and running up our national debt. Congress was not consulted as the Apollo Alliance prepared this bill, which was a true representation of the wolf-in-sheep's-clothing metaphor.

Another Soros company, The Center for American Progress, is also a partner of Agenda 21 and sustainable development through the guise of concern for the environment. It's just more of the same wolf dressed up like a gentle lamb. Here is a quote from Bracken Hendricks, a Senior Fellow at the Center for American Progress:

> "Local Governments are leading the nation in shifting to a low carbon economy today, in the face of federal inaction."

It's top down and bottom up. They couldn't get Congress to do what they wanted so they use the United Nations and unwitting mayors and city council members, most of who have no clue what the devil is doing through these evil sustainable developers.

According to Kuwaiti newspaper *Al-Jarida*, the *Washington Times*, Fox News, Breitbart.com, the *American Spectator*, Townhall.com and many other sources, President Obama has his sights set on becoming in charge of the United Nations as the secretary general. The current holder of that office, Ban Ki-Moon, has his term expiring at the end of 2016. Just twenty days later, Obama will be available. That position would be more to his liking as he considers himself a citizen of the globe more than a citizen of the United States. In addition, he wouldn't have to apologize for the U. N. like he does for America.

He could be proud of what he represents because he loves wealth redistribution, being an elitist and lecturing others as to how they should live for the collective. Now, he could become like a president of the whole world. It would be easy to transport his tools of the trade, because all he needs is a pen and a phone. He could continue to give speeches about Islam's contributions to the world, climate change, gun control, police brutality, and income inequality while lecturing to us that merit has no place in this world. He could bash America for its income inequality while he is staying in the most luxurious hotels and dining in the most exclusive restaurants. To his way of thinking, the best part of his new job would be the opportunity to destroy Israel.[12]

If Hillary is elected president, she will surely appoint judges to the Supreme Court who share her disdain for America. It will then be easy for us to lose our national sovereignty and therefore our Constitution and fall under the taskmaster of the Agenda 21 advocate, Secretary General Barack Obama. His first move would be for the U. N. police force to remove our guns. Success in that endeavor coupled with Obama's hate for America and Israel would be devastating. Fortunately, I believe that both of them will fail in their attempts to gain their new positions.

Obama addressed the General Assembly of the U.N. on September 27, 2015, extolling the virtues of the Agenda 21 update known as 2030 Agenda, the date in which they desire to fully accomplish their goal. Under President Obama, the U.S. adopted the "2030 Agenda for Sustainable Development" along with the other 192 nations in a unanimous vote. There was not one dissenting nation. Where was the news coverage of this? Here are some excerpts from Obama's speech of September 27, 2015 at the U.N. general assembly. These quotes were taken from the Whitehouse's own website.

"Today, we commit ourselves to new sustainable development goals, including our goal of ending extreme poverty in our world. We do so understanding how difficult the task may be. We suffer no illusions of the challenges ahead. But we understand this is something that we must commit ourselves to."

"Five years ago, I pledged here that America would remain the global leader in development, and the United States government, in fact, remains the single largest donor of development assistance."

"Today, I am committing the United States to achieving the Sustainable Development Goals."

What goals did he commit us to that he has not told the American people? There are population goals or agreed limits of people. They must be murdered.

"The Planetary Regime might be given responsibility for determining the optimum population for the world and for each region and for arbitrating various countries' shares within their regional limits. Control of population size might remain the responsibility of each government, but the Regime would have some power to enforce the agreed limits." -- Obama's science czar John P. Holdren, co-author of *Ecoscience*

If you read the speech from Obama, you will find that he makes it seem that he is a great humanitarian just wanting to help people in need. He fails to tell us that we all will be in need without our freedom and rights. We won't even have the right to life without approval from the elites. Oh, I forgot, we will have one right. We commoners will have the right to try and please our masters, the elite class.

CHAPTER EIGHT

AGENDA 21 COMPANIONS: COMMON CORE AND PLANNED PARENTHOOD

The Common Core initiative and the Planned Parenthood organization go hand and hand with the goals of Agenda 21. Planned Parenthood has the same philosophy of exterminating "undesirables" as does Agenda 21 and sustainable developers, and therefore, they protect one another. However, I believe Common Core was developed expressly for the purpose of fully implementing Agenda 21.

Common Core was the natural extension of No Child Left Behind, the Bush-era education reform law that tied federal funding for the nation's schools to new, mandatory standardized tests. Federal funding bribes have caused almost every state to sell out for Common Core. First, let's pull back the curtain on Common Core and other attempts to "dumb down" America through poor education, and then we will expose Planned Parenthood.

The website of Democrats Against U.N. Agenda 21 gives a good description of Common Core: "Common

Core is an integral part of UN Agenda 21/Sustainable Development: globalization is the standardization of systems. Whether the system is law enforcement or land use or government, the standardization, harmonization, and integration of all international methods of management is essential for total control. Education is the flash point for embedding system acceptance in all sectors of the population. Standardized propaganda is developed for pre-kindergarten to post graduate school; this is what is meant by 'Life Long Learning.' Breaking down traditional methods of learning in order to re-socialize the populace is the goal. Obedient, dependent people who are constantly being propagandized will provide the 'human capital' to fully implement UN Agenda 21/Sustainable Development. Regardless of the content of this nationalized and internationalized system of behavioral modification, the goal and outcome will be to fundamentally destroy the individual's rights."[13]

Common Core supporters claim that American school children are not prepared for the "twenty-first century global economy." That sounds like Agenda 21. Let me translate that for you. The truth is that until Common Core came along, American school children were more than prepared. They have to be weakened academically and full of ignorance if they are to swallow the garbage being hawked by sustainable developers.

The vast majority of people my age will never be fooled by such nonsense. However, if you start at the kindergarten level and then go through grade 12 spoon feeding Agenda 21 sustainability poison, bashing capitalism, extolling socialism and rendering American students incompetent in history, math, and science, they will have no choice but to go along to get along. Let's see. That will take thirteen years. Add that to 2016 and it's just in time for the 2030 Agenda. On top of that, if you keep feeding them the Kool-Aid through college and strap them with staggering tuition debt they become much easier to control.

Common Core proponents believe that children must be prepared to be proper Agenda 21 adults. Here is a quote from a UNESCO document called The Sustainable Development Toolkit explaining that less educated people use fewer resources. UNESCO is the lead agency of the U.N.'s "Education for Sustainable Development." UNESCO stands for the United Nations Educational, Scientific and Cultural Organization.

"Generally, more highly educated people, who have higher incomes, consume more resources than poorly educated people, who tend to have lower incomes. In this case, education increases the threat to sustainability."

Education is a threat to sustainability of a new world order. George Soros, one of the major financiers of the new world order, said, "The main obstacle to a stable and just world order is the United States." Therefore, the education in the United States must be diminished.

The stated goal of UNESCO is to integrate the principles, values and practices of sustainable development into all aspects of education and learning by encompassing the forty chapters of Agenda 21. This is the current goal of much of the curriculum of our federal government. For example, the entire purpose of second grade social studies is to transfer loyalty from the family to the government.[14] As Hillary would say, it takes a village.

From the Agenda 21 playbook, already deeply ingrained in the U.S. Department of Education, are the teachings of constructivism. In this concept "students construct their own understanding of reality, and realize that objective reality is not knowable." In other words, there is no real truth, not even the Word of God. New world order elites don't want men to be free so they can't know real truth, for it is the truth you know that makes you free. The existence of truth alone won't set you free. You must first know the truth and then the truth you know will set you free.

Below are some excerpts from a speech to the U.N. given by Arne Duncan, who, at the time, was the Secretary of Education of the United States. These remarks were given in an address to UNESCO on November 4, 2010 and taken from the government's own website at www.ed.gov

"Today, 37 states and the District of Columbia have already chosen to adopt the new state-crafted Common Core standards in math and English.... That is an absolute game-changer in a system which until now set 50 different goalposts for success. The Obama administration has an ambitious and unified theory of action that propels our agenda. The challenge of transforming education in America cannot be met by quick-fix solutions or isolated reforms. It can only be accomplished with a clear, coherent, and coordinated vision of reform. My department has been pleased to partner with the U.S. Agency for International Development to help ensure that our best domestic practices are shared world-wide.

The United States provides over a billion dollars annually to partner countries working on educational reform. Our goal for the coming year will be to work closely with global partners, including UNESCO, to promote qualitative improvements and system-strengthening."

Notice the words "transforming education in America." This is just a part of "transforming the United States of America" as promised by Barack Obama. There is nothing new under the sun. This is just another attempt at world domination like that of Joseph Stalin who stated the following: "Education is a weapon whose effect depends on who holds it in his hands and at whom it is aimed."

Common Core math (really the dumbing down of American math for Agenda 21) is called Connected Mathematics. Standard 3 from the teacher's guide entitled Mathematics as Reasoning, states that students "learn that mathematics is man made, that it is arbitrary, and good solutions are arrived at by consensus among those who are considered expert." Two plus two will not always be four because the consensus of experts might say that it is five.[15] Remember, there are no absolute truths. Students are trained to believe whatever their "expert" instructors tell them, no matter what. For example, in social studies the consensus might be that socialism always works out for everyone. Let's sing *Kumbaya*!

The teacher's guide tells us that they know that this way of teaching mathematics will not work very well in terms of academics. It says, "because the curriculum doesn't emphasize arithmetic computations done by hand, some students may not do as well on tests asserting computation skills."

Let's vote for people who are for a voucher system for education and let the American free enterprise capitalistic system make our educational system great again!

Now, let's look at Planned Parenthood. Let's start with a quote from its founder, Margaret Sanger from her book *Women and the New Race*.

> "The most merciful thing that a family does to one of its infant members is to kill it." – Margaret Sanger

Remember, Hillary Clinton said many times how she admired Margaret Sanger and that she especially admired her vision. Here is what Hillary Clinton said about Margaret Sanger upon accepting the 2009 Margaret Sanger Award from Planned Parenthood: "I admire Margaret Sanger enormously; her courage, her tenacity, her vision. I am really in awe of her."

Sanger's vision was to eliminate black people from the face of the earth. In *Pivot of Civilization*, Sanger referred to blacks, immigrants and indigents as "human weeds" and "reckless breeders" and "human beings who never should have been born."

Here is what Sanger said about her organization's goal to exterminate blacks:

> "We do not want word to go out that we want to exterminate the Negro population," she said, "if it ever occurs to any of their more rebellious members."

In a letter to Dr. Clarence Gamble, in December 19, 1939, Sanger shared her vision for the "Negro Project."

Below is an excerpt from the letter.

> *"It seems to me from my experience...that while the colored Negroes have great respect for white doctors, they can get closer to their own members and more or less lay their cards on the table, which means their ignorance, superstitions and doubts. We should hire three or four colored ministers, preferably with social-service backgrounds, and with engaging personalities. The most successful educational approach to the Negro is through a religious appeal."*

In February 1919, Sanger penned an article entitled "Birth Control and Racial Betterment." The quote below captures the essence of her message.

"And the government should "give certain dysgenic groups (those with 'bad genes') in our population their choice of segregation or sterilization."

Sanger's article "Plan for Peace" that appeared in April 1932 edition of *Birth Control Review* included the following:

> Article 1: The purpose of the American Baby Code shall be to provide for a better distribution of babies... and to protect society against the propagation and increase of the unfit.

> Article 4: No woman shall have the legal right to bear a child, and no man shall have the right to become a father, without a permit...

> Article 6: No permit for parenthood shall be valid for more than one birth.

Today, the vision of Margaret Sanger lives on thanks to Hillary Clinton and others in the Democrat Party. Bill Clinton appointee to the Supreme Court, Ruth Bader Ginsberg, said the following concerning the abortion issue:

> "Frankly I had thought that at the time Roe was decided, there was concern about population growth and particularly growth in populations that we don't want to have too many of."

According to the Guttmacher Institute, the former pro-abortion research division of Planned Parenthood, African-American women are five times more likely to choose abortion over white women. Planned Parenthood clinics are strategically planted in minority communities, targeting blacks and impoverished minority groups, and abortion remains the leading cause of death for the black community.[16]

If the Black Lives Matter movement really cares about saving black lives, they should protest outside of all the Planned Parenthood facilities across the nation.

In order for socialism and concepts like Agenda 21 to take control of our population, the mindset fostered by Planned Parenthood must be programmed into the minds of our young people. Make no mistake, these types of beliefs are demonic in origin and have been around since the fall of man. God wants us to be free and not controlled by some far off atheist bureaucrat that places no value on any human life except his own.

> "Birth control is nothing more or less than...weeding out the unfit." - Margaret Sanger

"But for my view, I believe that there should be no more babies." - Margaret Sanger

Here is what the Word of God says about bringing children into the world.

"As arrows are in the hand of a mighty man; so are children of the youth. Happy is the man that hath his quiver full of them: they shall not be ashamed, but they shall speak with the enemies in the gate." (PSALM 127:4-5 NKJV)

As we close our discussion about Planned Parenthood, consider these facts about today's Planned Parenthood. Women seeking help from Planned Parenthood are *never* advised to keep their baby. Not only that but they are almost never advised that the child be adopted. Of six thousand clinic visit records examined from a Texas Planned Parenthood clinic, only three were referred for adoption. They were all probably at the request of the mother and not suggested by Planned Parenthood.

In other words, their advice is almost exclusively, if not entirely, to have an abortion. In addition, Planned Parenthood does not offer the opportunity for an ultrasound. They don't want women to see that there is a baby inside of them, so they lie and call what's inside a mere blob of tissue.

From the Garden of Eden, to the Fabian Society, until today, Satan continually uses lies and deception to bring about death and destruction. Our Heavenly Father wants all those children to live and fulfill a wonderful and unique destiny.

"Before I formed you in the womb I knew you, before you were born I set you apart; I appointed you as a prophet to the nations." (JEREMIAH 1:5 NIV)

"You watched me as I was being formed in utter seclusion, as I was woven together in the dark of the womb." (PSALM 139:15 NLT)

"The thief cometh not, but for to steal, and to kill, and to destroy: I am come that they might have life, and that they might have it more abundantly." (JOHN 10:10)

CHAPTER NINE

HOW TO DEFEAT SATAN'S PLAN

Let's summarize the devil's plan to overthrow the United States of America and his strategy to establish a demonically controlled new world order without personal liberties for the common man. The devil expects to accomplish his plan through removing God out of our lives so government (ruling elites) can become our god controlling every aspect of our lives.

The devil always takes something beautiful from God and then distorts it. He is a counterfeiter. The Bible says that there will be no end to the increase of the government of God upon the shoulders of Jesus. The devil wants to direct man's ever-increasing government instead of Jesus directing God's government.

> *"For unto us a child is born, unto us a son is given: and the government shall be upon his shoulder: and his name shall be called Wonderful, Counsellor, The mighty God, The everlasting Father, The Prince of Peace. Of the increase of his government and peace there shall be no end, upon the throne of David, and upon his kingdom, to order it, and to establish it with judgment and with justice from henceforth*

even for ever. The zeal of the Lord of hosts will perform this." (ISAIAH 9:6-7)

Joseph Stalin, who was controlled by Satan, was a murderer like his father the devil and operated with the same strategy. Again, there is nothing new under the sun.

"Ye are of your father the devil, and the lusts of your father ye will do. He was a murderer from the beginning." (JOHN 8:44A)

Stalin's words reflected his thinking, just like his father the devil, and just like current Agenda 21 sustainable developers like Hillary Clinton and Barack Obama.

"America is a healthy body and its resistance is threefold: its patriotism, its morality and its spiritual life. If we can undermine these three areas, America will collapse from within." - Joseph Stalin

This is the plan of current depopulation sustainable developers. Their tactics are clear. They must control healthcare. That's the only way to have rapid depopulation. They must take away our guns. That's the only way to take away our property rights. They must take over education and nationalize it to focus all education around a phony environmental crisis.

They must make up and sell one bogus crisis after another. There is the environmental crisis. There is the food crisis as we are running out of food and all other resources. This justifies the need for a small population. They want to reduce the population and have us live like pre-historic cave dwellers. That's the only way they can totally control us.

At stake is our freedom to worship God and pursue a unique kingdom destiny, our property rights, such as the right to keep our homes and our land, our privacy rights, our national sovereignty, and even the most basic right—the right to live.

We have already lost many of our rights through onerous regulations that bypassed Congress and thus the people. Make no mistake about it. The progress made by Obama in his "transforming" of America will be hard to turn around. Obama, Hillary Clinton, and other sustainable developers will not give up or give in easily as revealed by Michelle Obama with these words in February 2008: "Barack will never allow you to go back to your lives as usual."

Many people wonder why Donald Trump has so much support despite his brash, overbearing style. Here is the answer: people want to see their country return to the greatness that they are used to. Their lives have been so disrupted by a failing economy and moral ineptness of our leadership, as demonstrated by giving Iran billions of dollars and nuclear capabilities that they will surely use to destroy the United States.

People just want to go back to their lives as usual, but the current crop of politicians won't be able to help with that. Trump seems to be the only one with enough backbone, lack of political correctness, and toughness to do it.

That is what I want. I want to see America greater than ever. I want to see our nation as truly one nation under God. So, it's time to stop talking about the problem and start talking about the solution and about the expectation by faith of God's deliverance of the U.S.A.

First, we need not be afraid. The devil will not win. I don't know exactly how God will bring the victory; I just know that he will. We, the church, will win because we will continue to do what God says we'll do and be who God says we are. We are the light and the salt of the earth; we are the Body of Christ, wearing the whole armor of God, wielding the weapons of our warfare and pulling down the strongholds of our enemy.

As revealed in the Book of Revelation, the agent of the devil, the Antichrist, fails in his attempt to subdue the world, even after the salt or preservative of the world, the church, is not in the world but with Jesus in heaven.

> "All attempts made by evil men to conquer the world have failed. The Antichrist will also fail. Jesus is the only one who will ever rule the world and bring peace. Research history from biblical times until now and discover how many different men have attempted to conquer the world. All were ungodly and failed miserably. Satan himself cannot take the earth from God, so he keeps looking for the right human, one whom he can use to attempt this theft." - Hilton Sutton, *The Book of Revelation Revealed*

The reason I am exposing Agenda 21 and its supporters is not because I'm afraid that they will fully succeed, but because I don't want to lose any more freedoms. On the contrary, I want to have our freedoms fully restored. I want all people to know that God is for them and that the devil wants to take their freedoms away. We should know who the real enemy is and what his strategy is.

"For we wrestle not against flesh and blood, but against principalities, against powers, against the rulers of the darkness of this world, against spiritual wickedness in high places." (EPHESIANS 6:12)

"Lest Satan should get an advantage of us: for we are not ignorant of his devices." (2 CORINTHIANS 2:11)

How does God want to use his people to defeat the plans of our enemy? Let's start with what I call the dominion mandate. We have read in Genesis chapter one where God gave dominion to man. "Let them have dominion." Man lost that dominion through sin, but this dominion has been restored to the body of Christ through the blood of Jesus. Now, the church must exercise the dominion that God has mandated that we operate in on this earth.

Dominion is the purpose for man's creation and existence. Mankind, under God's leadership, was created to rule over the earth. We were created for his pleasure and it is his pleasure for his children to rule. Why does it bring God pleasure when we exercise our God-given dominion? Because we do it by faith, and faith pleases God. In doing so, we receive more of our kingdom inheritance, which is pleasing to God.

"Fear not, little flock; for it is your Father's good pleasure to give you the kingdom." (LUKE 12:32)

This is an area in which God's people need to improve and we will. If we are supposed to have dominion, why is there all the trouble and chaos in the world? Something must not be going exactly right. Do you suppose many of God's people are ignorant of their dominion mandate?

Please indulge me and let's use our imagination for a moment.

Suppose a visitor from another planet came to observe the earth for a while. He was told to observe those who called themselves Christians. After his lengthy time of observation of God's people, he was told that the book they follow has a mandate given to them. Considering what he detected, he was to fill in the blank to complete what their book mandated. He was given the following: Let them _____.

After pondering all that he watched of the church, he returned the paper he was given. It read as follows. Let them <u>drink coffee.</u> Suppose you explained that the Bible says "Let them have dominion." Then you asked him if he saw much of the church taking dominion over sickness and disease, the world system, and the power of the devil. He would probably say something like this. "I didn't see a lot of that, but every time they got together they sure did drink a lot of coffee."

In general, Christians have not been taught enough about the dominion mandate. As a result, many have been destroyed.

> *"My people are destroyed for a lack of knowledge."*
> (Hosea 4:6a*)*

We need to realize that just because God gave us dominion, it will not automatically happen. We should rule as God would rule, as we are his representatives on earth. How is this accomplished?

We "call things that are not as though they were."

In order to take authority or dominion, we must use the spoken word. When we call things that are not as though they were, we act like our Father God. By your words, you will either act like God or the devil. You will either express the will and Word of God or you will express the deception and lies of the devil. Your words have power.

> *"Death and life are in the power of the tongue: and they that love it shall eat the fruit thereof."* (PROVERBS 18:21)

We live in two realms. There is the unseen spiritual realm and the seen natural realm. The best way to get your tongue right is to stop looking at the seen world and start looking at that which is not seen, namely, the promises of God.

> *"So we fix our eyes not on what is seen, but on what is unseen, since what is seen is temporary, but what is unseen is eternal."* (2 CORINTHIANS 4:18 NIV)

The Word of God is eternal; it never changes and is seen through the eyes of faith. The natural or things that are seen with the natural eyes are temporary or subject to change. They change when we find a promise in the Word of God and we believe it in our hearts and we speak it with our mouths and walk like it is done because it is. The seen must change when the Word of God is believed and spoken, because the Word cannot change.

That is how our nation will stop moving away from God and start moving back toward God. We need to believe and say that this nation is turning to God, even when our natural eyes tell us that it is not. That is what "calling things that are not as though they were" is all about. The natural seen world will change to what we say it is. To believe that takes faith and that is what pleases God.

As discussed in the introduction, we should prophesy (believe and speak) to the church in America to live and become an exceedingly great and effective army. We also discussed the sowing and reaping aspect. We saw that the Democrats mocked God in their 2012 convention and that God will not be mocked because we reap what we sow. The Democrats' plan for socialism shall fail. We should concentrate on sowing good seeds that glorify God.

In the natural, we should cling to the Constitution and to the Second Amendment of the Bill of Rights concerning the right to bear arms. We should vote for those who defend the Constitution, who value the life of an unborn child, who support Israel, and who seek to follow God. We should not vote for anyone who wants to give voting rights to illegal aliens, even if it's in the future.

We should pray for our nation to turn back to God. We should pray for liberty and pray for the peace of Jerusalem. We should individually obey God, win souls, speak the truth in love, and demonstrate the love of Jesus. After you have done all that, then leave the rest to God.

> *"Therefore put on the full armor of God, so that when the day of evil comes, you may be able to stand your ground, and after you have done everything, to stand."* (EPHESIANS 6:13 NIV)

One thing that the leaders of Agenda 21 and those who

support sustainable development have in common is that they don't want to serve people. Instead, they want power over people so that they can be served by others. There are many people in our government today who are there for what they can get and not what they can give. I declare, in Jesus' name, that there is going to be a turnaround in our nation and even around the world. This is the promise in the Word of God that I believe and I am speaking it. I would love for you to join with me. The term "nations" below represents the current United Nations.

"The nations have fallen into the pit they have dug; their feet are caught in the net they have hidden. The Lord is known by his acts of justice; the wicked are ensnared by the work of their hands. The wicked go down to the realm of the dead, all the nations that forget God." (PSALMS 9:15-17)

Remember, King Saul sought to bring about David's death to keep David off the throne, but it was Saul's death that gave David the throne. The Egyptian army attempted to drive the Israelites into the Red Sea to drown, but it was the Egyptian army that drowned in the Red Sea. Haman built gallows in an attempt to hang Mordecai so Haman could be exalted, but it was Haman that was hanged on his own gallows and Mordecai was exalted.

"That same day King Xerxes gave Queen Esther the estate of Haman, the enemy of the Jews. And Mordecai came into the presence of the king, for Esther had told how he was related to her. The king took off his signet ring, which he had reclaimed from Haman, and presented it to Mordecai. And Esther appointed him over Haman's estate." (ESTHER 8:1-2 NIV)

Agenda 21 and the socialist elite class desire power and control over people. They put together plans to control us little people. I say according to Psalms 9:15-17, that whatever power they do have will be stripped away and they will eventually be seen as a scourge on this nation and mankind. The things they exalt like socialism and Planned Parenthood will be exposed and abased.

Like Haman, their own deeds will destroy them. What they meant for others will come back on them. They will lose their freedoms and privileges. Those things they wished to destroy that are precious to God like capitalism, freedom loving people, and the freedom to worship God, will be fully restored and exalted in the United States of America. Politicians who want to serve will be recognized and given honor, and those who want to be served will be removed from office.

I further prophesy in the name of Jesus that God will expose corruption for all to see and the people will be astonished. I declare it and decree it in the name of Jesus. If we will believe the promises of God we will win. Don't give up, don't quit. The only way to lose is to quit.

> *"Let us not become weary in doing good, for at the proper time we will reap a harvest if we do not give up."* (GALATIANS 6:9 NIV)

Child of God, I believe in you. I believe in you because my Heavenly Father says he believes in you and he cannot lie. I believe you won't quit and we will see the victory in our land. We will truly see one nation under God. I say with confidence that Jesus is Lord over the United States of America. I believe the church will prevail.

I want to encourage and challenge the body of Christ in the United States as Churchill challenged the people of Great Britain during the Second World War. The bombing of London by the Germans was a picture in the natural of the demonic bombs coming against our nation today. As a result, I offer this challenge to the church of Jesus Christ in America today.

Let us therefore brace ourselves to please God through our faith words and so bear ourselves in obedience, that if Jesus should tarry for another 1,000 years, men will still say of the American body of Christ, "This was their finest hour."

ENDNOTES

1. Sutton, Hilton, As the United States Goes, So Goes the World (New Caney, Texas: Hilton Sutton World Ministries), 29.
2. https://centurean2.wordpress.com/2008/10/27/they-word-socialism-was-not-to-be-used-for-sure-it-aint/
3. https://en.wikipedia.org/wiki/Fabian_Society
4. www.docfoc.com/chronology-of-mass-killings-during-the-chinese-cultural
5. https://en.wikipedia.org/wiki/Cloward%E2%80%93Piven-stategy
6. https://www.youtube.com/watch?v=+9dnLgTo6MU
7. http://www.aipnews.com/talk/forums/thread-viewasp?tid=187.
8. www.democratsagainstunagenda21.com/iclei-when-they-say-local-they-mean-it.html
9. https://www.youtube.com/watch?v=AZzSEOgbAaA
10. Ibid.
11. Ibid.
12. www.spectator.org/65145_obama-could-become-president-whole-world/
13. www.democratsagainstunagenda21.com/common-core-is-agenda-21.html
14. https://www.youtube.com/watch?v=AZzSEOgbAaA
15. Ibid
16. www.liveactionnews.org/7-shocking-quotes-by-planned-parenthoods-founder/

Other Books by
DAVID HOPE

Available at www.davidyanezbooks.com

The Goodness of God

Inhabiting Eternity on Earth

Was Jesus a Socialist, or a Capitalist?

Keep Knocking

Visit us at
WORDS OF LIFE CHURCH

David Hope is the Senior Pastor of Words of Life Church, a non-denominational, Spirit-filled family church in Humble, Texas. Join us for service the next time you're in the Houston area.

Words of Life Church
7811 FM 1960 East
Humble, TX 77346

Service Times:
Sundays @ 10:40am
Wednesdays @ 7pm

www.WordsofLifeChurch.net

www.ingramcontent.com/pod-product-compliance
Lightning Source LLC
LaVergne TN
LVHW051131080426
835510LV00018B/2343